Along for the Ride

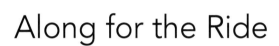

Along for the Ride

Getting Your Money Working for You Through Real Estate and Stocks

Owen Bigland
www.owenbigland.com
t: @owenbigland
Youtube: OwenBigland

ISBN: 1542673364
ISBN 13: 9781542673365
Library of Congress Control Number: 2017900974
CreateSpace Independent Publishing Platform
North Charleston, South Carolina

Acknowledgements

I dedicate this book to my beautiful wife, Kumal for all her love and support.

I'd like to thank Nick Raithel, my friend, colleague, and writer. No one has contributed more to this book. From the very beginning he helped brainstorm and organize the book. He then helped craft every chapter and perfect every word. If books were movies, this would be known as a "Nick Raithel Production".

Table of Contents

Introduction

"To be an investor you must be a believer in a better
tomorrow"

- BENJAMIN GRAHAM, RENOWNED INVESTOR AND MENTOR TO
WARREN BUFFET

■ ■ ■

Who is this guy?
This "Owen Bigland" character.

The one listed on the cover, as author of this book.

That would be me.

Speaking (weirdly) in the third person. But only to echo your own thoughts.

Let me start by saying that your thoughts are justified.

You're right to question me because I haven't properly introduced myself.

Sure, there's an "About the author" snippet on the back cover. But that's hardly a proper intro. Nor would you expect it to be. For a short paragraph is rarely (if ever) enough to convey a complete picture of a person.

If you're in doubt, just look at online dating. It's probably the ultimate example of why a single paragraph just isn't enough. Far too often, a few glowing sentences in a profile end up being horribly inaccurate. The person who sounded like a "bombshell" or a "hunk" online doesn't live up to these expectations in person. It's underwhelming, to be sure. And it reinforces why a single paragraph can't fully represent another person.

Recognizing this, I want to now go beyond my "About the author" snippet. Expanding it for you, with a brief yet valuable look at who I am.

The picture I'll paint for you here can hopefully resolve your questions. Most importantly, I hope it proves to you why I'm qualified. Why I can speak to you as an expert on the topics in this book. And why you should listen to me.

To paint that picture, let's go back in time. Back to mid-February 2013. I still remember that particular day like it was yesterday.

It was a Sunday. Cold and rainy too. The kind of day you'd never expect to find any sunshine. Yet around 9 AM, the sun came out for me. Figuratively speaking.

It appeared for me as I sat at the desk in my home office. Sitting there, my mind was on fire. It blazed with the natural "high" from an early morning workout. As the endorphins fired, I worked with stunning clarity on my taxes.

Clarity caused confusing calculations, for example, to melt before me. I cut through them, as the proverbial hot knife does through butter.

Calculations like the dividend income from my stocks. A total comprised of all of my dividend income, as paid by the dozens of Canadian, U.S. and international companies that I own stock in. A diverse lot, I might add, made up of companies from Pepsi to Apple to Royal Bank to Disney. And sitting in a portfolio that I built from the ground up over the past twenty-five plus years.

Normally, such a calculation would give me a headache. Yet this morning, it was painless. I had no difficulty locating all the requisite info and churning out my dividend income.

Next I moved on to my real estate portfolio. As with my stock portfolio, my real estate portfolio had also been built one property at a time, starting over twenty years ago.

I added up all the income (rent checks each month) that I received from all my tenants. From that total, I then calculated the expenses on each property.

Those expenses came from properties that I owned and rented out to tenants. My expenses included things like maintenance fees, repairs, property taxes, and in some cases - interest on mortgages (a deductible expense).

Gathering those figures, again with surprising clarity, I was able to see my total expenses from real estate for the last year. I then subtracted this figure from a separate total, the rental income I had earned for the year. What remained was my total net real estate income for the year.

Not to bore you with math - but there's one more calculation to mention. It's total passive income. The total that appears when income from "passive" sources is added together.

For me, those "passive" sources were real estate and stocks. In each case, I did not have to actively work for every single dollar I received. Both sources were therefore "passive" since they would pay me regardless of what I did.

On that rainy Sunday morning, I entered my total net real estate income for the previous year into Excel. Then I keyed in my total dividends received, from all the stocks I owned, for the same period. And finally, almost for dramatic emphasis, I paused. My finger hovered above the "Enter" key, for a split second. Then, as the moment passed, I hit enter, summing the two totals.

That's when I saw it. You would have seen it too. Bright sunshine in defiance of the morning rain clouds. The sunshine was, again, figurative. Yet it shone just as brightly to me as the real thing.

The source of my "sunshine" was the figure produced in that last calculation. My net passive income. It shone before me now as I realized this total was more than enough to ensure I never had to work another day in my life.

I could choose to work, of course. But even if I didn't, I'd still be able to maintain my current lifestyle. A lifestyle that included eating out at restaurants, training at the gym, and keeping a nice car. I could continue doing those things, along with taking 2 to 3 vacations per year. All without ever working again for anyone, for any reason.

Thinking about that bright future, I felt tears forming in my 80 year-old eyes.

Actually I didn't. Because I wasn't 80 years old. Not even close. I was half that, in just my mid-40's. Not an elderly person by any means. Nor was I at the point when most people even dream about retirement. I was young. A "baby", compared to people in those latter age ranges.

Can you imagine this feeling?

Not as I would have felt it. But as you might feel it. In your own life.

It's the feeling that comes upon hitting the "cross-over point". A point at which the income from your investments produces enough cash flow to cover all of your expenses. All of them. So you can choose to never, ever...ever work again.

Keep in mind that this cash flow (at the "cross-over point") is just what my portfolio is producing. I'm not having to sell any of my assets - real estate or stocks. This is passive income from the portfolio. Where my underlying assets continue to appreciate, getting more valuable each year.

You can reach that point too.

It's well within your grasp.

Without buying a "magic system" for $19.95 (plus shipping).

Make no mistake - hitting your cross-over point is indeed a magical experience. But there's no "magic" formula to get you there.

What it takes instead are patience and consistent action. Directed at your goal over decades. (Decades!)

How can I be so sure?

For one thing, there's the fact that I've achieved my cross-over point. So when I speak of what it takes to get there, you can rest assured in the fact that I've actually done it. That separates me from others who are all talk. Those armchair advisers who tell of how to reach the "cross-over point", yet haven't gotten there themselves.

I'm also confident of what it takes because of other personal experiences. Experiences that reinforce the value of patience, consistent action, and an unwavering long-term perspective.

One of those experiences came in 2000. It's another experience which, like the "cross-over point", is burned into my mind. The setting, though, was markedly different.

I was at La Guardia Airport in NYC. Preparing to catch a flight home to Vancouver. Sometime in August.

If you've traveled in August, you can probably imagine what it was like. Crowds of people. The norm for many airports. Yet amplified in August by everyone taking their annual summer vacation.

Crowds are great for those who run airlines and airport kiosks. But they're a major pain for those of us who don't enjoy crying babies or slow-moving "herds" of people.

As I maneuvered through both at La Guardia, my eyes suddenly fell upon something entirely different.

Something I'd been expecting, yet a welcome surprise all the same.

It was the August issue of Men's Workout Magazine. As a long-term fitness enthusiast, I've always enjoyed this magazine. At that point in my life, though, the publication took on added significance. For I was actively engaged in those years as an amateur bodybuilder.

Over a span of many years, I'd devoted myself to training day in and day out at the gym. That's actual training, by the way, rather than merely yelling and clanging weights. Some "bodybuilders" may be able to train this way. Yet I never found them at competitions.

What I did find at competitions was, eventually, personal success. It wasn't overnight at all. Over thousands of nights, maybe. Just not overnight or miraculously fast. Bodybuilding - like reaching your "cross-over point" - doesn't work that way.

The success does come, though. I'd gotten a truly satisfying taste of it in 1993. The year I won my first bodybuilding contest. A moment when years of time and sacrifice crystallized into a magical result.

Winning my first contest gave me the vision I needed to reach another magical point - that August day in 2000 at La Guardia Airport.

The latter day was magical, in its turn, because it marked a new kind of achievement. I had "won" here by getting on the cover of Men's Workout Magazine.

I mention this to you now, not to brag. Let me be very clear on that. My life will go on, regardless of who knows or doesn't know about the magazine cover or my other achievements.

My goal in telling you of these things is, as noted earlier, to give you a sense of who I am. And why you should trust me in giving advice.

I hope my efforts are succeeding in both those respects. Hopefully you do feel more confident on who I am and why I'm credible.

In the case of bodybuilding, my credibility comes from the fact that I've been successful in it. With the magazine cover and contest wins. Those successes, in turn, allow me to speak as an authority on the value of patience, consistent effort, and a long-term focus. For those 3 ingredients brought me success both in bodybuilding and financially, with my "cross-over point". I have, in other words, successfully "walked the walk" in two seemingly different disciplines.

Does that make me credible?

Probably. But I can't expect you to trust me just yet. Let me give you one last experience to truly cement my credibility. It's an experience that like the earlier two, is also unforgettable.

This third experience differs, though, by not being a single moment. It's an experience comprised of many moments. Those moments were, collectively, during the 2008-2009 financial crisis. A time when the world's financial system seemed to "meltdown".

Those were dark days. Darker still than the rainy February morning later, in 2013.

For me, the darkness came from watching my portfolio get cut in half. Many of the careful investments I'd made over the years were suddenly crushed, losing tremendous amounts of value.

This collection of painful moments was the equivalent of being repeatedly punched in the gut. The market dealt me these crippling blows during the period from 2008-2009. I wasn't the exception, of course. Yet that didn't make it any less painful.

As my stocks "bled" profusely, though, I forced myself to look for the silver linings. The opportunities to profit, even amid the chaos.

Many other people were doing just the opposite. Jumping ship. Some of them even relinquishing their self-employment for "safe", "stable" 9-to-5 jobs.

I couldn't join them. No matter how bad it got. No matter how many days I felt the crushing doubts rise within me. Quitting wasn't for me. So I held the majority of my investments and soldiered on, even searching for buying opportunities.

Eventually, the clouds did lift. The financial markets "limped", then "walked", and finally "ran" forward again. Resuming their old ways at last, after the downturn.

Standing tall with the remnants of my portfolio, I watched as the market steadily rebuilt it. Allowing me to regain my earlier position and then venture past it to the "cross-over point".

You already know how the story unfolded. I did indeed make it back from the financial crisis to hit financial independence (a.k.a. the "cross-over point") in 2013.

This gives me the right, therefore, to advise you to stay the course. Because when all hell broke loose in 2008/2009, I stayed the course. It was painful and nerve-wracking but I didn't crack.

What may not be as apparent is that at no time, did I ever work multiple jobs or crazy-long hours. In fact, anyone looking at me in those years, or my 20's to mid 30's would be disappointed. I never really paid a lot of attention to "getting rich" during those times. I was too busy having fun and enjoying life.

That's not to say I wasn't also investing. I did that too. I was working hard, paying myself first, and systematically investing. This meant buying stocks every month or so when I had money. And buying investment properties when I could afford them.

Yet these investments were not my single all-consuming life focus. I knew, as I'll advocate in this book, that financial independence is a long-term objective. It's the result of steadily rolling assets together, over the decades, to create an unstoppable "snowball".

Your figurative snowball will come together.

So why not enjoy some hot cocoa, sledding, and other analogous winter fun along the way?

I've written this book to help you do just that.

If you're ready to see how exactly it's done, let's get this show on the road.

Come along for the ride, beginning now with Chapter One.

One

It's not all about real estate

"Ninety percent of all millionaires become so through owning real estate."

- ANDREW CARNEGIE, STEEL TYCOON AND "ROBBER BARON".

"Buying and holding Vancouver real estate sets the table for so many other financial opportunities down the road."

- OWEN BIGLAND, AUTHOR AND VANCOUVER REALTOR (OWENBIGLAND.COM)

■ ■ ■

Don't be fooled.

This book is NOT about real estate.

It may sound like a real estate book, from the title.

And it may be positioned like a real estate book, from where you find it in the bookstore.

But ultimately this book is NOT about real estate.

Not by a mile.

The truth is that the book you're about to read is focused on something bigger.

Financial independence.

That's the true focus.

And real estate?

Well, that's part of how you become financially independent.

Part of how you do it. Not the complete formula. Just one component. Regardless of whatever you may have heard in infomercials or at a weekend seminar.

No need to point fingers. It's just that most of the voices on real estate, have it all wrong. Never mind the fact that many of them have never been realtors. Or successful for that matter.

No, the real problem is that much of the conversation presents real estate alone as the solution. Do some tricks in real estate and voila, you'll be set financially.

As a licensed realtor and an investor of over two decades, let me be the first to say - I wish it were that easy. For I know nearly every "trick" there is...and then some. If it were really just a case of making a few clever moves, as the gurus claim, there would be far more real estate millionaires.

But the truth is that real estate doesn't work like that.

Don't get the wrong idea, though. You can make substantial sums of money from real estate.

I have.

But without the right knowledge; any money you do make from real estate is unlikely to last. You may or may not end up broke. But you'll certainly never achieve financial independence.

Not unless you have the right knowledge.

And this book aims to provide you with some of it.

That's my goal as the author. As I mentioned before, I'm a realtor by trade. So you can bet that much of the discussion in this book will be on real estate. Yet as you've also been reminded again and again, this book is NOT about real estate. Not really. I want to talk instead about how to achieve financial independence, with real estate as the first step. It's this distinction that separates my book from the others you may have seen.

Half of those other books are probably about personal finance. Written by people like Suze Orman, Dave Ramsey, and (if you're a millenial) Ramit Sethi. These are the books that focus on financial independence alone. Crack them open and you'll find topics like cutting down on your credit cards (often literally) and saving money for retirement.

On the other side are the books that deal purely with real estate. "Books" is actually a pretty generous way to describe them. Most are not even up to the title. Instead, they tend to be hype-driven pamphlets, masquerading as reputable guides and trying to push you into attending a seminar.

Ok, maybe that's a bit harsh. There are definitely some real estate books on the market that are well-written and valuable. Yet these books are few in number and tend to be written for people already in real estate. That makes such books relevant for me, a realtor, but of little use for you, the reader without real estate experience.

Considering all this, I've decided to create a "middle ground". With this book, my goal is to bridge the gap between the money management books and the real estate ones. I want to create that "missing link" that shows you how to move toward financial independence by following realistic, hype-free real estate strategies.

This book will not, in other words, be anything resembling a "get rich quick" book. If that's what you're after, stop reading now. Put this book down and return to hunting for the non-existent "silver bullet" to riches. But if that's not you, keep reading. Stay with me and you'll be delighted by what you find. I'm going to spend this book teaching you a simple process that leads, over decades, to wealth.

Decades. Not tomorrow. Not the week after. Not next week. Not even next year. We're talking twenty-five to thirty years or more. A period which seems like an eternity today. Yet one that will be over in seemingly the blink of an eye. (Just ask any senior citizen!)

If you can patiently follow my process for that period, you'll end up financially independent. Curious what the process is? I don't want to spoil the book. But I can give you a preview now.

My process is to build and maintain a cash-producing wealth machine. You do that by buying and holding quality real estate and equities. These assets appreciate over time, while also providing you with a steady stream of cash - in the form of rent checks and dividend checks. As the cash arrives, you then redeploy it into the purchase of more real estate and equities.

Overall, my process is a simple rinse and repeat. You do some work up front to create an investment "snowball", as Warren Buffet would describe it. Then you sit back and let time take care of the rest. The decades do the heavy lifting for you, turning your portfolio into a "muscle-bound" freak.

As an added perk, the process I'm describing doesn't require you to quit your day job. You simply spend a few hours each week monitoring your holdings and looking for the next purchase. Do that and the process is 100% guaranteed to create wealth.

The wealth you create will be lasting too. Meaning you won't ever have to worry about running out of money in retirement. The money won't dry up because you won't ever have to sell your assets. Not unless you want to. You can keep the assets and live off the cash flows they produce.

Cool, huh? It's not how most people support themselves in retirement. The masses tend to follow the so-called "4% rule". When doing so, they support themselves by selling approximately 4% of their assets each year. Can you see how they run the risk of ending up with no money? Especially as seniors enjoy ever longer lifespans.

Living longer should be a cause for celebration, not a reason to despair. With the simple process I detail in this book, the despair will never come. Money concerns will never dampen the enthusiasm with which you blow out the candles on your birthday cake.

It's a simple process. But it's not easy. The difficulty comes primarily in being patient. Most people struggle to do that. They act as their own worst enemy, derailing any progress toward financial independence.

If you can just be patient, you will become financially independent. I know that for a fact. My own financial independence came in my mid-forties. I know too, of some people who achieved this independence in their mid-30's.

Notice how I say "financially independent" rather than "rich". That's an important distinction. To be clear on the difference in terms, let's define them both.

For our purposes here, "financial independence" will be defined as never having to work for money at any point over the rest of your life.

Achieve financial independence and work becomes optional. There won't be an economic "gun" to your head compelling you into labour each day. Any work you do engage in will be done purely by choice.

Compare this position to being "rich".

Actually, it's difficult to make a comparison because "rich" is a very vague term. Think about it. When you speak of wanting to be "rich", what exactly do you mean?

Do you mean "rich" in the same way that a steak is "rich" in flavour? If so, then you'd probably define "rich" as having an overabundance of something.

Something? Or money?

That's up to you as well.

For "rich" doesn't just mean money. You could be "rich" in opportunities. Or you might be "rich" in the sense of having abundant talent.

For argument's sake, let's say we're limiting "rich" to just money.

Ok, but how much money?

A hundred dollars? That's "rich" to the 2.8 billion people that the U.N. says live on less than $2 per day.

A million dollars? That's "rich" in America, where The Daily Mail reports annual salaries are an average of $54,450.

A billion dollars? That's "rich" for the 14.6 million people worldwide that Fortune says have assets of at least one million dollars or more.

Get the picture? The amount of money that it takes to be "rich" is relative. So when we say "rich", let's define it simply as having more than enough money to spend on all of the things you want. This definition reflects the loose nature of being "rich".

With this definition in hand at last, we can finally compare "rich" versus "financially independent".

Looking at the two side by side, the differences are readily apparent. "Rich" is specifically tied to having money. So long as you have the money, you're "rich".

Financial independence, on the other hand, is about more than just having money. A person can be "financially independent" if they have a specific amount of money in the bank. Yet the same person can also be "financially independent" if they have less money, but earn passive income from investments each month. Both cases would make a person "financially independent", since they would not be required to work for a living.

So which would you rather be?

Rich?

Or financially independent?

Decide for yourself. But I'd strongly suggest you choose financial independence. It's a more permanent state than just being rich. And in this book, I'll show you how real estate can be the first step to help you get there.

Before we continue, I want to be clear on why real estate deserves your attention. Of all the possible ways you could get started toward financial independence, why this one?

Forget for a moment that I'm a realtor. Look only at the cold, hard facts of real estate.

Regardless of where you look, you'll find that in the long-term, real estate nearly always trends upward. I'm not making this up either. All you have to do is take any long-term price graph of 25 to 50 years, for properties in a major North American city.

Pick a U.S. city. Any city. From New York to New Orleans. From San Antonio to San Francisco. No matter what city you pick, you'll see that properties have consistently risen in price over the past decades. Not only risen, but risen on a scale resembling Mount Kilimanjaro.

This isn't just an American thing either. Look at Canada. In a city like Vancouver, my home city, property prices have also risen consistently from one decade to the next. You can see this in the graph on the following page.

The graph shows the unprecedented appreciation in detached homes versus condos and attached properties (i.e. townhomes). Looking at the graph, the appreciation is staggering.

What explains it?

Dirt.

That's what you're buying, after all. And they're not making any more of it.

What they are making more of are multi-family units (condos). Condos are being built in droves due to re-zoning and development for more density. Yet as we've said, there's only a limited amount of dirt available. So in order to have room for more multi-family units (condos), detached homes are being removed. The shrinking supply of detached homes causes the demand for them to increase. The result is that your "dirt" becomes ever more valuable

A final point on this graph. As the title indicates, it's a graph for real estate. But what if it was the graph for a publicly-traded company. Suppose Vancouver Real Estate was a public company (trading as "VRE", for example), on the S&P 500. Then it would be one of the most successful companies of all time. Most real-life companies can only dream of having their stock charts look this good. What CEO wouldn't want their company's growth to be a beautiful, slow ascent with a moonshot finish? Especially, as the graph shows, for detached homes. It's the stuff of corporate dreams. But it doesn't have to be. The CEOs and you, as well, can wake up and actually live those dreams. With real estate.

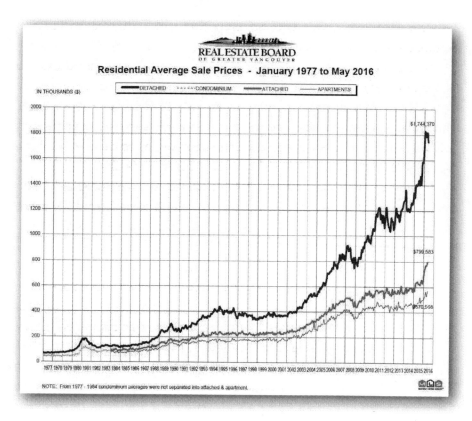

REAL ESTATE BOARD
OF GREATER VANCOUVER

Residential Average Sale Prices - January 1977 to May 2016

IN THOUSANDS ($)   DETACHED   CONDOMINIUM   ATTACHED   APARTMENTS

$1,744,370

$799,583

$570,568

NOTE: From 1977 - 1984 condominium averages were not separated into attached & apartment.

Real estate is the answer because it consistently increases in value. That increase may not come this year. Two, three, or five years from now; a property's price may still not have increased. The price may even have decreased, as a result of market fluctuations. But fluctuations are almost always short-term. Meaning that over a long-term window, usually at least a decade, the price of real estate will always increase. (Just look at the Vancouver graph here or a comparable one for your city!)

This increase is tied to several factors. First, populations continue to grow. There are more Americans today, for example, than in previous decades. Any population, especially a growing one, needs housing. Yet in a major city, there is only so much land on which housing can be built. So as the population grows and demands more housing, the supply of available, metropolitan-area housing is bound to decrease. This conflict between supply and demand inevitably causes a long-term increase in real estate prices.

At the same time, real estate prices also trend upward due to the fact that nearly everything tends to get more expensive over the years. And we do mean everything. From consumer goods (clothing, soft drinks, electronics, etc.) to items related to real estate (building materials, labour, insurance, etc.). This is the reason why you may hear older people complaining about how little you can get for a dollar these days.

Choose real estate and you can profit rather than complain. You'll profit if you recognize that the rising prices aren't to be feared. Embrace them instead as natural inflation, something that happens in most developed economies and always will. Then look to your own property. You'll see that the inflation works to your advantage because it increases the fixed cost of building nearly any type of property. Houses, condos, apartments; all become more expensive to build with the steady rate of inflation. Even with inflation averaging just two to three percent annually, your property's value is still bound to increase.

There's a third factor too. One that further drives real estate prices upward. It's foreign capital. Money flowing from other parts of the world into the North American real estate markets. The money is coming now that, as economist Thomas Friedman declared, "the world is flat". A "flattened" world makes it easier for people in other countries to see all of the available real estate opportunities. All of them. Not just in China, for example. But everywhere.

In China's case, many of its wealthy have found and fallen in love with Vancouver. It's not hard to see why they're smitten. Vancouver is a hub of international cultures, an outdoor lover's paradise, and a former Olympic host. The city is also consistently ranked by The Economist as one of the world's most livable.

As money comes into Vancouver, from China and other countries; there's more competition for properties. Locals ("Vancouverites") are now competing in the real estate market against potential buyers from around the world.

Vancouverites aren't alone in facing foreign competition. The competition between locals and foreign buyers for real estate is playing out across North America. You're likely to find it in any major coastal city. On the west coast, the competition plays out in cities like Vancouver, Seattle, San Francisco, and San Diego. Back east, you'll find it's locals "versus" foreign buyers for real estate in cities like Toronto, NYC, Washington D.C., and Miami.

All of this competition pushes real estate prices up. Dramatically. A two bedroom condo in Vancouver, for example, is no longer worth $400,000. The condo would normally cost that much if based on local salaries. Now that the world is "flat", however, buyers with substantially greater salaries are eyeing the same properties. So our two bedroom condo skyrockets in price to a cool $1 million. It may go up even more, given the unprecedented state of real estate in Vancouver. This kind of price appreciation is not normal and I can't say exactly where it will go. Yet even with the uncertainty, you should still see real estate as an opportunity that trends upward overall.

There's more to real estate than just rising prices, though. Another of real estate's allures is that it sets you up for three financially-liberating opportunities.

The first of those opportunities is leverage. It's a magical thing. Just how magical? Well, with leverage you could, for example, make a down payment of $20,000 and get control of a $400,000 condo in a major city. For the mathematically-challenged, this equates to paying just 5% of the condo's total price in order to fully control it.

In our example here, you'd still have to pay down the cost of the condo over time. But remember that over a long enough window, the price of the condo - like nearly all big city real estate - is bound to increase. So despite whatever money you have to pay, you've still gained control of a money-making asset for far less.

The takeaway from this example is that real estate lets you do things with your money that would normally be impossible. You can't walk into Starbucks, for instance, and offer to pay 5% now for a $4 Frappuccino.

Even if you had perfect credit, the barista would still laugh you out of the shop.

The same goes for many, many more things. Excluding, of course, real estate. In real estate, your 5% down payment has a chance to be taken seriously and not seen as a punchline. Provided of course, that you have the financial wherewithal, qualifying for a mortgage from an approved lender. Assuming you do, real estate provides you with incredible leverage opportunities - the kind that you're unlikely to find elsewhere.

Apart from leverage, real estate also affords you a second major opportunity. This is the opportunity for tax-free capital gains. If you purchase a property as your principal residence, you enjoy tax-free capital gains on it. This means that as the property's value increases, you pay no taxes on the increase. All growth (a.k.a. capital gains) is 100% tax-free.

To illustrate this opportunity, picture buying a $400,000 condo today as your principal residence. In thirty years, that residence could easily be worth $2 million. Were you to then sell it, the $1.6 million in capital gains would go to you fully tax-free at the time of sale. You'd have become a millionaire, just from sitting on your ass(et).

The third major opportunity real estate sets you up for is passive income. Passive income means that you earn money without having to work for it. Real estate can provide you with opportunities for passive income, provided that it's an investment property you rent out to tenants. In that case, you would receive rent payments from the tenant, regardless of whether you did anything at the property. Naturally, you could be a good landlord and visit the tenant on a regular basis. But even if you didn't, your rent checks would still come in for as long as you had tenants. This is the magic of passive income. It helps to facilitate financial independence since your income no longer depends on you having to work. You can passively earn the money you need to live, as opposed to actively working for it.

With all this talk about leverage, capital gains, and passive income, you might (hopefully) be coming around to real estate. If you're beginning to "see the light", you may be wondering whether real estate is a good idea right now. In this economy. Shouldn't you give it some time given that [insert event affecting the economy] has just happened?

In response, I'd encourage you to stop thinking about what's a "good" or "bad" time to enter the market. Timing the markets like this is ultimately for fools. And not fools like the guys at renowned investment firm, "The Motley Fool". No, fools in the sense of people who think they're somehow smarter in the short-term than the market.

If you try to outsmart the market in a short-term window - whether that's a few months or a few years - you're going to waste your own time. Your "careful" avoidance of the market may lead you to miss out on hot properties for sale, or get worse interest rates after they've increased.

Speaking of interest rates, here's an example of how they affect affordability - especially when the rates are at record lows. (You can do similar examples at Calculator.net.)

In our example here, suppose you took a $400,000 mortgage in 2007. That year the average five-year fixed term interest rate was 6.5%. As a result, your monthly payments on the mortgage would have been $2,700.83. These payments would go primarily toward interest on the mortgage for the first fifteen years. Then from year fifteen onward, each monthly payment would begin to pay down more principal than interest.

But it's not 2007 is it? So let's look at it based on interest rates today (2016). Today the same rate we just saw is now 2.1%. It's fallen nearly 4% in roughly a decade. The drop matters to you because it will affect the amount of your monthly mortgage payments.

Recall that under the 2007 rate (6.5%), your payments each month were $2,700.83. With today's (2017) 2.1% rate, however, you'll only pay $1,714.96 per month. That's a savings of almost $1,000 per month. Imagine what you can do, from a wealth-building standpoint, as a result of the savings. At the very least, you'll have an easier time making each monthly mortgage payment. The payments become much more affordable to you due to the lower interest rates.

"But wait, there's more!" Remember the principal on your mortgage? That ten ton load standing between you and the end of the mortgage.

Lower interest rates allow you to accelerate the rate at which you can pay the principal down. You don't have to wait fifteen years before you begin paying more principle than interest each month. You can start doing that right in the first year of the mortgage.

Will interest rates drop even lower? Maybe. But there's not much space for them to. Zero is the limit. Barring some isolated - truly isolated - exceptions in Europe, negative interest rates just don't happen. This means today's interest rates are at a record low. That's in comparison to both 2007, and earlier decades too. I remember, for example, paying around 11% to 12% interest on my first property in the late 80's. 11% to 12% percent then, versus just 2.1% now? Yeah, this is kind of a big deal. Bigger still when you recognize that low interest rates drive property prices. The current record-setting prices in both Canada and the USA are a direct result of all-time low interest rates.

Considering interest rates, I would strongly advise you to take action in the real estate market now. As I said before, it's utter folly to believe you can outsmart the market and wait till a "perfect" time.

I've personally seen the folly of waiting in my own market. Here in Vancouver, people around me are constantly talking about how our real estate market is a "bubble". For the past twenty years, I've heard repeatedly that the market is bound for a crash. People have warned me to get out while I can, and insisted that they need to "wait this one out".

Do you think I listened to all this talk about a Vancouver real estate "bubble"? No. And neither did the market. Barring some occasional "hic-cups", the Vancouver real estate market has proceeded to climb three-hundred percent over the last two decades.

A crash may be coming, at some point. What's more likely is that we'll continue to see corrections. Real estate markets tend to correct them-selves every three to four years, anywhere from five to fifteen percent. Vancouver's last correction was in 2012, when property values in our real estate market dropped approximately eight to twelve percent. Writing this now, in early 2017, we may be due for another correction.

Yet that's a reality of being in nearly any investment scenario, whether we're talking real estate or the stock market. Markets correct, markets crash, and markets soar. Markets aren't always going up or down either. Sometimes they stay flat too. Any direction is possible really, for a short-term (i.e. 1 to 5 years).

The key, though, is to be in the game. It's like Woody Allen famously said, "eighty percent of success is showing up". If you want to succeed at real estate, you've got to show up. You've got to leave the sidelines and enter the game. And commit to being in the game for the long-term. All nine innings of it. Or in our case, twenty-five years or more.

But you don't have to do it alone. Let me teach you how to enter the real estate business and use real estate to achieve our ultimate goal of financial independence. We'll do it together using this book.

Are you in?

Then join me in the next chapter, where we'll make sure you're NOT making the #1 mistake most people make when thinking about real estate.

Two

Winning the mental game of real estate

"Real estate cannot be lost or stolen, nor can it be carried away. Purchased with common sense, paid for in full and managed with reasonable care, it is about the safest investment in the world."

- FRANKLIN D. ROOSEVELT, U.S. PRESIDENT

"Time is your friend; impulse is your enemy"

- JOHN C. BOGLE, VANGUARD FOUNDER

■　■　■

Your jaw would have dropped. Mine certainly did. Standing inside this house as rain dripped through the ceiling, mildew clung to the floorboards, and a platoon of ants marched up the walls.

Was this really the same house? The one that looked so inviting on the outside. Freshly painted shutters. A well-kept front lawn. Not to mention a great location on the ever-popular Vancouver Westside.

This house seemed to have everything going for it. That was the reason I'd dropped everything to come for a showing. I couldn't believe the house was still for sale.

Until, of course, I went inside. Then the truth was readily apparent. This place had too many internal issues to ever be a move-in house. It was a tear-down house and nothing more. A buyer would have to be blind and deaf to think otherwise.

Looking back on this episode, I believe it captures the essence of why many people are not financially independent. Like the house, we may look fine on the outside. Good job. Good credit. Savings in the bank. Everything that should put us on track to financial independence.

But only on the outside.

Inside, in the inner reaches of our minds, it's a different story. Like the house, we have too many internal issues to ever achieve our goal. We may have "sold" ourselves on financial independence. But those mental issues need to be resolved if we ever wish to actually close the deal.

Now "mental issues" can be a broad and even offensive phrase, so let's be clear on what it means here. I'm not suggesting you have a mental disorder like schizophrenia. Instead, my point is that your mind may be rife with certain roadblocks or barriers. These obstacles are so strong that they can lead to self-sabotage. So you may appear to be on the road to financial independence, yet never get there due to persistent internal problems.

My goal in this chapter is to help you overcome one of these internal problems. I believe it's the largest and most serious of the bunch. The problem to which I'm referring is the "trader's mentality".

The trader's mentality comes from the world of stocks. In that world, people are accustomed to stocks being bought and sold in a short period. Sometimes, that period is a few weeks. At other times, it can be as brief as a few minutes. But it's almost always short. With some exceptions, the average trader isn't looking to buy a stock and then sell it in ten years. Traders tend to be focused instead on the here and now. What stocks can be bought and then sold (i.e. "flipped") in the shortest possible time for the highest possible profit.

You can't blame them for thinking this way. The trader's mentality makes perfect sense on Wall Street, where the markets are whizzing around at breakneck speeds. In that kind of climate, short-term thinking can literally pay off.

The problem, though, is that the trader's mentality is often transplanted into other fields. Fields that are nothing like stock trading.

In my work as a realtor, I see this mistake time and again. People look at properties with the eyes of a stock trader. They don't understand that a trader's strategy of quickly buying and selling ("flipping") stocks won't work on houses.

The reason is that real estate properties are fundamentally different from stocks. A property like a house is not some invisible thing that a company can arbitrarily issue more of. Instead, the house and nearly any other piece of real estate is physical and limited in quantity. Because of these differences, it's a far bigger deal to buy and sell real estate than stocks. Property inspections have to be done. Banks have to be notified and then approve financing. Insurance has to be worked out. And all that is just the tip of the proverbial iceberg. So many items have to be handled in a real estate transaction that the process often takes months.

Buying and selling stocks, by contrast, can be done in a matter of seconds. This means that a trader could sell off his entire portfolio of stocks in a few short minutes. Good luck doing that in real estate. A real estate portfolio, made of multiple properties, would take months or even years to sell off. And it would also be more expensive to sell than the stock portfolio. Transaction costs for selling a stock portfolio might be a few hundred dollars. Compare that to real estate where costs include capital gains taxes, agent commissions, and legal fees. Add those real estate costs up and you're looking at tens of thousands of dollars.

Given all of these differences, it's a major mistake to think about real estate using the short-term, trader's mentality. You're better off approaching real estate with the investor's mindset.

When you think like an investor, you focus on the long-term. This is perfect for real estate, since it's a market that doesn't go up every year. Stocks don't go up every year. But neither does real estate or any other market (antique cars, art work, wine, etc.).

Real estate prices do increase, though. It's just that the increase happens over spans of at least eight to ten years. That time frame favors the investor, since they don't mind waiting.

The investor's mindset is also preferable in real estate because it allows you to be "recession proof". To illustrate what I mean, here's an example from 2008.

Back in early '08, I saw people in Vancouver buying condos in pre-construction developments for over one million dollars each. The building, however, had yet to be built. By the time it was completed, in late 2009, the same condos had lost nearly 10% of their value. These million dollar units were now worth a "measly" $900,000 each.

Watching this, I could only shake my head at what came next. Like clockwork, many of the condo owners began to reveal their trader's mentality. These owners had likely bought the condos with the intention of quickly "flipping" them. Their plans had not included a scenario where the condo lost 10% of its value. To see this happening must therefore have been downright terrifying. To the traders.

To the investors, though, the drop in value wouldn't mean much. Sure, the value of their unit was down $100,000. But it would only be a loss if they sold at that point. Any investor that looked at the condo as a long-term investment and stayed in the game...well, they would have a chance. For as I keep saying, the real estate market in major cities always goes up over a long enough window. If you can just wait out a bad real estate market, holding what property you have, then you essentially become "recession proof". One of the best ways to do this is by making a property, like a million dollar condo, your principal residence. That gives you a plan "b", letting you ride out market turbulence and benefit from real estate's inherently forgiving nature. We'll be talking about how to do that later in this book.

For now, let's continue on in our discussion of the investor's mindset. I want to make sure you're fully clear on how to think like an investor and not a trader. Otherwise, you enter the real estate game at a distinct disadvantage.

At this point, you know that a long-term, investor's mentality is key in real estate. But how long is "long-term"?

If it's an investment property, it's forever. Or at least ten to twenty years. My goal with these is to hold it, use a tenant's rent to pay my own expenses, pay off the mortgage eventually, and then just collect passive income stream.

If it's a principal residence, "long-term" there (principal residence) is going to mean approximately eight to ten years, at a minimum. And the longer the better.

I'd recommend this latter time frame because it gives you enough of a runway to survive market fluctuations. Fluctuations are a virtual certainty since the real estate market inevitably moves to correct itself. Take comfort, though, in knowing that most real estate markets tend to "bounce back" quickly after a fluctuation. So don't be afraid to wait.

Wait if you need to, but don't get the impression that you should never sell real estate. I'm not advising you to sit on properties forever. You could do that and support yourself through passive income from tenants. But it's not the only way. Selling is always an option, and there are definitely times when it will make sense for you.

Common examples here include divorce, relocation due to a job, and no longer needing the same amount of space. Selling your property might also make sense if you had a "hungry" developer, who would pay far more than the property was actually worth. This latter scenario is the kind of dream that many a home owner hopes for. Whether your developer ever arrives or not is another story. Don't let a dream (or greed!) delay you if you're considering selling. Your local real estate market can easily experience another fluctuation while you're on the fence. Interest rates are an example of this. So are government efforts to curb foreign investment - an issue in Vancouver, where much of our real estate market is driven by Chinese investors. Whatever the cause, your market can come crashing down without warning. When this happens, you may be forced to stay in the market, despite your own desire to get out.

The bottom line? If you're thinking of selling, and it makes sense personally, do it!

Another point I want to make is that you should never time the markets with your principal residence. What I mean is, don't try to be real estate's equivalent of Houdini.

Houdini? Yes, as in Harry Houdini, the legendary magician. Houdini could throw away the keys to a building and then enter it without difficulty. You, on the other hand, aren't so lucky. If you sell your principal residence, thereby "throwing away" the keys to it; you probably won't be able to get back in. That's not an issue if you sold and intended to leave for good. But some people aren't like that. These are the people who try to be Houdini. They believe you can sell your principal residence at peak price, rent for a bit, and then re-enter the game later when the market changes. Only it doesn't always work that way. Trust me. I know from experience.

Back in 2011, real estate prices were up. Way up. At the time, I saw many wannabe "Houdini's" selling their principal residences. Believing they could time the markets with super-human accuracy. Were they on to something? It could have looked that way by the following year (2012). That year we had a correction. The intoxicating real estate prices gave way to a kind of "hangover" period, a time when the market seemed to sober up. Prices fell somewhat, leaving those wannabe Houdini's to feel they had acted correctly. Now they just had to wait for the reverse. Let the market continue to correct and prices to continue falling. In time, prices would reach an ultimate low point. Then these boneheads could buy their principal residences back.

Yes, I just called them "boneheads". And that's because of what happened next. 2013 arrived and the real estate market suddenly took off again. Turns out the correction was just a short-term one. Prices were not going to fall any further. Rather than fall, prices shot up, once more hitting the stratosphere.

Those who had sold their principal residences must have felt like boneheads. Can you blame them? Their clever scheme to outsmart the market didn't work out so well. The market may have appeared to die, but it was only playing possum. As it returned now, these humiliated speculators found themselves left in the cold. On real estate's sidelines. Unable now to afford their principal residences.

The moral of the story here is to not try and time the markets. Especially when you're doing so with your principal residence. It's a recipe for disaster.

No matter what you hear predicted on the news.

That's a final aspect of the long-term, investor's mindset. Filtering out who you listen to. If you're going to remain focused on long-term windows of time, you can't be getting distracted by "flash in the pan" news stories. Such stories flare up, with excitement and alarm, before quickly burning out. They may have some value to stock traders. But the stories carry no value whatsoever to you, in real estate with an investor's mindset. Filter them out.

And don't stop there. Filter out much of what you listen to elsewhere. Like the advice from "experts". Funny, isn't it, how many "experts" there are today? Everyone seems to be one. Fortunately, not all "experts" are successful in their own right. This criteria, success, can help you to suss out who's legit.

In addition, you want experts (*no quotes, since they are actually experts) who are transparent. Advice from an expert real estate investor, for example, is of no use to you if the expert won't open up. If that expert won't be transparent on their thoughts, actions, and results; you're better off listening to one who will.

While we're on the subject of transparency, I invite you to visit my video blog. Here's a link – YouTube.com/OwenBigland.com

Visit the blog and you'll see that I practice what I preach. My blog gives expert advice on real estate, while also being fully transparent. In doing so, I make no secret of my own thoughts, actions, and results. Go on, visit the blog and see what I mean...

■ ■ ■

Back from the blog?

Or did you even visit?

Either way, we're now at the close of this chapter. As we end, I want to remind you again to approach real estate with a long-term vision in mind. Stop thinking, for example, about what a property will be worth in a year. Think instead about what that same property's value will be in ten or fifteen years.

Along with that, I encourage you to remember why we're even talking about real estate in the first place. Our discussion on real estate stems from the fact that it's the first step toward financial independence. In this chapter, we've looked at the mindset necessary for success in real estate. A mindset that will help you to be as strong internally as you are externally.

Now that we've covered mindset, let's look at how exactly you get started in real estate. What's the first thing you do? Like the very first thing?

The answer is in Chapter three.

See you there!

Three

Your first move

"Unless you want to stay living in your parent's
basement forever, with your ping-pong table
and your Bon Jovi posters on the wall - you need
to make a commitment early to save and buy
your first condo. It's the first step on the ladder
towards financial freedom."

- OWEN BIGLAND

■ ■ ■

You don't want a witty introduction, do you?
I started writing one over breakfast today. Scribbling it on cardboard from a cereal box. It was "witty" and you might have laughed.

But that introduction now sits at the bottom of a trash can. I threw it away mid-sentence because it's not what you want.

If you've read this far, you're probably eager to get into specifics. So let's not put this off any longer. The last thing I want to give you is another book that teases big ideas but never explains how to actually implement them.

We've already alluded to our own big idea - financial independence. In this chapter, we'll cut to the heart of the matter. You'll discover the step-by-step specifics of how to make your first forays into real estate. Those forays, in turn, will put you on the path toward long-term financial independence.

To begin the discussion, let's answer the question we ended Chapter Two on. If you'll recall, Chapter Two ended by asking, what's the first thing you should do in real estate?

Here's your answer: buy a condo or an apartment.

Buying a condo or an apartment should be your first step for two main reasons.

First, you need a place to live. It's really that simple. Even if you're a corporate "slave", pulling hundred hour work weeks. And even if you're a free-spirited partier, who stays out all night. The slaves, the partiers, and everyone in between, all need somewhere to live. Somewhere you can eventually return to, no matter what time it is. Buying a condo or an apartment gives you that place.

Buying?

Yes, buying. As in purchasing and then owning the place where you live. That may seem like a mistake to you, if you've always rented. Perhaps you view renting as more cost-effective.

Today it's not. But twenty years ago, you'd be right. At that time, renting really could save you money.

What changed?

Interest rates.

They affect the mortgage you'll take out when buying a condo or apartment. The higher the interest rate, the more money you'll have to pay each month on your mortgage.

Looking back a few decades, we can see that interest rates have plummeted. In the early 80's, for example, interest rates stood at 20%. By the mid-nineties, though, rates had dropped to 11-12%. And today, interest rates now sit at roughly 2%.

To understand interest rates better, check out the following two tables.

Table 1 - Mortgage Calculator at 2.1% Interest Rate

(as taken from Mortgage Calculator @ www.calculator.net)

Mortgage Calculator

Home Price	$500,000	
Down Payment	20	%
Loan Term	25	years
Interest Rate	2.1	%

Monthly Pay: $1,714.96

House Price	$ 500,000.00
Loan Amount	$ 400,000.00
Down Payment	$ 100,000.00
Total of 300 Mortgage Payments	$ 514,487.55
Total Interest	$ 114,487.55
Mortgage Payoff Date	Sep. 2041

Annual Amortization Schedule

Annual Schedule

	Date	Beginning Balance	Interest	Principal	Ending Balance
1	9/16 - 8/17	$ 400,000.00	$ 8,282.08	$ 12,297.44	$ 387,702.58
2	9/17 - 8/18	$ 387,702.58	$ 8,021.36	$ 12,558.16	$ 375,144.42
3	9/18 - 8/19	$ 375,144.42	$ 7,755.05	$ 12,824.47	$ 362,319.99
4	9/19 - 8/20	$ 362,319.99	$ 7,483.14	$ 13,096.38	$ 349,223.63
5	9/20 - 8/21	$ 349,223.63	$ 7,205.45	$ 13,374.07	$ 335,849.58
6	9/21 - 8/22	$ 335,849.58	$ 6,921.90	$ 13,657.62	$ 322,191.97
7	9/22 - 8/23	$ 322,191.97	$ 6,632.30	$ 13,947.22	$ 308,244.76
8	9/23 - 8/24	$ 308,244.76	$ 6,336.57	$ 14,242.95	$ 294,001.83
9	9/24 - 8/25	$ 294,001.83	$ 6,034.56	$ 14,544.96	$ 279,456.90
10	9/25 - 8/26	$ 279,456.90	$ 5,726.18	$ 14,853.34	$ 264,603.58
11	9/26 - 8/27	$ 264,603.58	$ 5,411.23	$ 15,168.29	$ 249,435.31
12	9/27 - 8/28	$ 249,435.31	$ 5,089.61	$ 15,489.91	$ 233,945.42
13	9/28 - 8/29	$ 233,945.42	$ 4,761.18	$ 15,818.34	$ 218,127.10
14	9/29 - 8/30	$ 218,127.10	$ 4,425.78	$ 16,153.74	$ 201,973.38
15	9/30 - 8/31	$ 201,973.38	$ 4,083.26	$ 16,496.26	$ 185,477.14
16	9/31 - 8/32	$ 185,477.14	$ 3,733.47	$ 16,846.05	$ 168,631.13
17	9/32 - 8/33	$ 168,631.13	$ 3,376.29	$ 17,203.23	$ 15,142.93
18	9/33 - 8/34	$ 15,142.93	$ 3,011.52	$ 17,568.00	$ 133,859.96
19	9/34 - 8/35	$ 133,859.96	$ 2,639.03	$ 17,940.49	$ 115,919.50
20	9/35 - 8/36	$ 115,919.50	$ 2,258.65	$ 18,320.87	$ 97,598.63
21	9/36 - 8/37	$ 97,598.63	$ 1,870.19	$ 18,709.33	$ 78,889.31
22	9/37 - 8/38	$ 78,889.31	$ 1,473.48	$ 19,106.04	$ 59,783.28
23	9/38 - 8/39	$ 59,783.28	$ 1,068.37	$ 19,511.15	$ 40,272.15
24	9/39 - 8/40	$ 40,272.15	$ 654.67	$ 19,924.85	$ 20,347.31
25	9/40 - 8/41	$ 20,347.31	$ 232.20	$ 20,347.32	$0.00

Table 2 - Mortgage Calculator at 6.5% Interest Rate

(as taken from Mortgage Calculator @ www.calculator.net)

Mortgage Calculator

Home Price	$500,000
Down Payment	20 %
Loan Term	25 years
Interest Rate	6.5 %

Monthly Pay:	**$2,700.83**
House Price	$ 500,000.00
Loan Amount	$ 400,000.00
Down Payment	$ 100,000.00
Total of 300 Mortgage Payments	$ 810,248.59
Total Interest	$ 410,248.59
Mortgage Payoff Date	Sep. 2041

Annual Amortization Schedule

Annual Schedule

	Date	Beginning Balance	Interest	Principal	Ending Balance
1	9/16 - 8/17	$ 400,000.00	$ 25,805.54	$ 6,604.42	$ 393,395.60
2	9/17 - 8/18	$ 393,395.60	$ 25,363.24	$ 7,046.72	$ 386,348.90
3	9/18 - 8/19	$ 386,348.90	$ 24,891.31	$ 7,518.65	$ 378,830.26
4	9/19 - 8/20	$ 378,830.26	$ 24,387.75	$ 8,022.21	$ 370,808.09
5	9/20 - 8/21	$ 370,808.09	$ 23,850.49	$ 8,559.47	$ 362,248.65
6	9/21 - 8/22	$ 362,248.65	$ 23,277.28	$ 9,132.68	$ 353,115.98
7	9/22 - 8/23	$ 353,115.98	$ 22,665.65	$ 9,744.31	$ 343,371.67
8	9/23 - 8/24	$ 343,371.67	$ 22,013.05	$ 10,396.91	$ 332,974.77
9	9/24 - 8/25	$ 332,974.77	$ 21,316.74	$ 11,093.22	$ 321,881.57
10	9/25 - 8/26	$ 321,881.57	$ 20,573.82	$ 11,836.14	$ 310,045.44
11	9/26 - 8/27	$ 310,045.44	$ 19,781.12	$ 12,628.84	$ 297,416.62
12	9/27 - 8/28	$ 297,416.62	$ 18,935.34	$ 13,474.62	$ 283,942.02
13	9/28 - 8/29	$ 283,942.02	$ 18,032.94	$ 14,377.02	$ 269,565.01
14	9/29 - 8/30	$ 269,565.01	$ 17,070.06	$ 15,339.90	$ 254,225.14
15	9/30 - 8/31	$ 254,225.14	$ 16,042.73	$ 16,367.23	$ 237,857.93
16	9/31 - 8/32	$ 237,857.93	$ 14,946.59	$ 17,463.37	$ 220,394.57
17	9/32 - 8/33	$ 220,394.57	$ 13,777.03	$ 18,632.93	$ 201,761.67
18	9/33 - 8/34	$ 201,761.67	$ 12,529.15	$ 19,880.81	$ 181,880.88
19	9/34 - 8/35	$ 181,880.88	$ 11,197.72	$ 21,212.24	$ 160,668.65
20	9/35 - 8/36	$ 160,668.65	$ 9,777.06	$ 22,632.90	$ 138,035.79
21	9/36 - 8/37	$ 138,035.79	$ 8,261.31	$ 24,148.65	$ 113,887.16
22	9/37 - 8/38	$ 113,887.16	$ 6,644.04	$ 25,765.92	$ 88,121.26
23	9/38 - 8/39	$ 88,121.26	$ 4,918.44	$ 27,491.62	$ 60,629.76
24	9/39 - 8/40	$ 60,629.76	$ 3,077.30	$ 29,332.66	$ 31,297.11
25	9/40 - 8/41	$ 31,297.11	$ 1,112.82	$ 31,297.14	$0.00

These two tables each show mortgage amortization, based on the same $400,000 mortgage amount.

Table 1 is based on today's interest rate of 2.1%. Table 2, by contrast, shows the rate you would have paid around 2007 (6.5%).

Look at the monthly payment today versus in 2007. Today, you'd pay $1,714 per month to buy that condo. In 2007, that same condo would have cost you $2,700 per month.

Also, look at the principal vs interest ratio. Today, you're paying off more principal than interest right from year one. Back in 2007, though, it would take you fifteen years to reach that same cross-over point.

Nice, but that's not all. The best part is when you look at "Total of 300 Mortgage Payments" in the upper right-hand of the table. This amount reveals that in today's terms, your total cost (interest + principal) on a $400K mortgage will be $514,487.55 after 25 years.

Yet in 2007 that $400K mortgage would have a total cost after 25 years of $810,248.59. So in 2007 terms, it would be more than double the cost of the original loan amount.

Also, if you want to see something really ugly, add in nine or ten percent for the interest rate. That's what I was paying around 2000. My total mortgage cost then translated to three times the original loan amount. Now that's a sight for sore eyes!

But not today. And this is the power of low interest rates. It's the main reason why real estate prices are where they are at today, at all-time highs. It's also another reason why renting long-term in a low-interest rate environment makes no sense.

With rates having fallen, there's often little difference now between what you'd pay each month for a mortgage and what you'd pay for monthly rent.

Don't believe me? Come to Vancouver, my home city. There, in a suburb called New Westminster, you'll find one-bedroom apartments starting around $175,000. Imagine that you purchased one of these apartments. In doing so, suppose you made a down payment of $10,000 and took out a mortgage of $165,000.

At the present interest rate (2.55%), your monthly payment on the mortgage might be $744. You'd also be paying an additional $225 for monthly maintenance fees, and then $80 per month in property taxes. Together, that amounts to about $1,050 per month total.

For that amount ($1,050), there would be virtually no difference between buying and renting. No difference that is, in terms of how much you'd be paying each month. There would, however, be a profound difference between what you were getting for your money each month.

With renting, your monthly payments would keep you in the apartment. Pay for the month to stay for the month. And so on. Until you either moved out or were evicted. At which time, you'd leave the apartment with nothing to show for all of the money you'd paid in rent.

If, on the other hand, you were to buy the apartment; then you'd be in an entirely different position. As we said, you'd be on the hook for mortgage payments each month. Yet these payments would be going to pay down your mortgage. Each payment would move you a bit closer to owning the apartment outright. Eventually, you'd pay off the entire mortgage and no longer have to make monthly mortgage payments.

At that point, your $744 per month would disappear. All you'd be responsible for would be the monthly maintenance fees and the property taxes. It would be like the landlord decided to stop charging rent. Only in this case, with buying, all of those "rent" payments would have gone toward helping you fully own an asset (the apartment).

The bottom line is that you're better off buying an apartment or condo than renting one. Knowing the advantages of buying, let's continue our discussion of why buying a condo or apartment should be your first move in real estate. One reason we already gave was that you need a place to live.

Going forward, another reason is opportunities for leverage. As noted in Chapter One, leverage means being able to do things with your money that would normally be impossible. Real estate gives you ample opportunities for leverage. Chapter One demonstrated this with the example of buying a condo. We saw that you could pay 5% of a condo's total price in order to fully control it. That means you could make a down payment of just $25,000 to acquire a $500,000 condo.

If this example doesn't leave you feeling excited about leverage, here's another. Suppose that the price of the $500,000 condo increases to $550,000. It's not a stretch to assume this because nearly all real estate eventually increases in value. With the new $550K price, the condo is now worth $50,000 more than when you bought it. Since you put down $25,000 as your down payment, you've made a 100% return on your investment in the condo.

A 100% ROI? The thought gives people in other fields goosebumps. Look on Wall Street, for instance. Some traders on the Street would give their kidneys for a 100% ROI. And that's not necessarily a figure of speech. A 100% ROI really is out of reach for those guys. To them, it often seems as elusive as the Loch Ness Monster or Bigfoot.

Good thing we're not trading stocks. We're in real estate, a field where a 100% ROI is not only possible, but also inevitable - depending on how many years you hold a property. In our field, a 100% ROI could even come within a year of acquiring a property.

Should that happen, don't sell your property. You may be tempted to sell, since it means - in theory - that you can claim the 100% ROI. Fight the temptation, though. You really don't want to sell at this point. Trust me. We're still in the first inning. And there are plenty of innings to go.

Selling is a bad idea because you won't get the full 100% ROI. It may look like there's a $50,000 payday waiting for you if you sell. Yet selling entails numerous expenses. Capital gains taxes would be one, if it's not your principal residence or if you've lived in it for less than one year. Others would include realtor selling commissions, and legal fees. After these expenses, your $50K payday could look more like a $35K payday.

But wait, there's more...

You've also taken a huge step backward. By cashing out as soon as your property increases in value, you're now without any assets. Back to square one. With a little more cash than when you started. Yet no closer to building a framework for long-term financial independence.

Sorry to beat you over the head with this. Especially after we spent Chapter Two covering the need for long-term thinking and an investor mindset. I just want you to be mindful of the temptation that can arise when your first real estate investment begins to bear fruit. That's always an exciting time. I see it as analogous to growing tomatoes in a backyard garden. At the first blush of red, it's tempting to pick the tomatoes and eat them. Yet if you can just wait a few weeks, your tomatoes will taste infinitely better. So too with real estate, where a good ROI today can be even sweeter years later.

Ok, so we're clear now on the need to hold the condo or apartment that you buy. But why a condo or apartment? Why not a house?

We can start with affordability. That's a definite reason NOT to buy a house. When situated in an urban center, houses ("detached homes") generally cost more than nearby condos or apartments.

The price difference comes from the fact that the house is detached. Being detached, the house sits on its own land. It's not on shared land, as is the case with apartments and condos.

Now "land" for a house in the city could just mean a small square patch. We're not exactly talking about acres and acres. But it's land all the same. And as a wise man once said, they're not making land any more.

With a finite supply of land, there's less space for houses. This shortage results in fewer houses, especially in major cities, and higher demand for those houses. All of which makes houses more expensive than apartments and condos.

Given the high prices, detached houses in a major metro area are probably out of your price range. At least if you're just getting started in real estate. And that's perfectly OK. You can get started with the money you do have by purchasing an apartment or condo.

Understand too, that "purchase" doesn't mean you instantly pay the entire price for a property. Instead, you can make a down payment (i.e. an initial upfront payment) that's a percentage of the total price. We saw this in our discussion of leverage, where a $25,000 down payment could get you into a $500,000 condo.

Whatever your down payment for a condo or apartment ends up being, it'll still be less than for a house. Houses have higher down payments because their overall prices are higher.

I'm not making that up either. You can see the proof on Vancouver's east side. A basic house there costs between $1.5 and $2 million. Don't worry, though, you won't have to cough up a few mil to move in. All you'll need is the down payment. A tidy "little" sum of $250,000. No worries, right? In fact, the money's probably sitting in your bank account right now.

Or not.

No, most of us don't have anything near $250K freely available. That's why people gamble and play the lottery. And it's why in real estate, it's far easier for you to buy an apartment or condo. For these latter types of property, you're looking at a down payment of perhaps $15,000 to $25,000.

Fifteen to twenty-five thousand dollars may still be out of reach for you right now. But with focus and a plan, you can get to it in no time.

For the purposes of this book, I'm not going to tell you how exactly to get your down payment. It wouldn't make sense for me to. You know your own personal situation far better than I do. Besides, this isn't a book on budgeting. Our focus here is on real estate. So let's assume you're capable and creative enough to come up with the down payment.

On that assumption, let's now work through the step-by-step process for purchasing your first property. Our discussion will center on how you buy that initial apartment or condo.

Thinking about the process, let me begin by giving you an unusual suggestion.

Don't look at any real estate listings.

Not in the beginning.

Those listings are meaningless to you until you've clarified the terms of your mortgage. Without clarification, you won't know how much money a bank or lender will allow you to borrow. And absent that "little" piece of information, you'll have no idea which of the advertised properties are in your price range.

To get clear on the terms of your mortgage (i.e. how much you can borrow), you'll need to do two things. First, pick up the phone and call the bank or lending institution that you'd like to borrow from. When someone picks up, explain that you want to get a mortgage. That should trigger a flood of questions from the person at the other end. You'll be asked about your income, debts, and other financial matters. All in the interest of pre-qualifying you for the mortgage.

Answer those questions and you'll be given a general estimate for how much money you can potentially borrow. Whatever the estimate is, recognize that it's neither official nor binding. You still need to get formally pre-approved. Until that happens, any estimates are just that... estimates.

As for pre-approval, you'll do that by visiting your bank or lending institution. Visiting allows you to prove to the banker or lender that you're telling the truth about your finances. The truth will emerge as you provide income tax returns, bank account information, and proof of your ability to make a down payment.

If all of your information checks out, a bank or lending institution can then pre-approve you for a mortgage. With the pre-approval, you'll receive a letter stating the exact dollar amount that you can borrow.

Knowing how much you can borrow is a game-changer. This knowledge changes everything because it gives you a frame of reference. You're no longer guessing wildly about what you might be able to afford. Instead, you know with certainty what is and isn't in your price range.

Apart from knowledge, getting pre-approved also enables you to begin working with a realtor. That's because nearly all realtors want to see that you've been pre-approved.

Speaking as a realtor myself, I can say that pre-approval gives us realtors confidence. We can see you're in a position to afford properties we suggest. Plus, we like the fact that you went and got the pre-approval letter. Getting the letter shows initiative on your part. It's validation for us that you're not just all talk. You've actually gotten up and taken the first steps yourself toward buying a property. Seeing this, it's easier for us to believe you're a serious buyer.

On the subject of realtors, I'd encourage you to choose yours carefully. For the truth is that you're probably not starved for choices. Most of us can find a few realtors. Just contact a friend of a friend, ask for a referral, or read the names off some local "for sale" signs. Any of those actions can bring you into contact with realtors.

But not all realtors are the same. Like any profession - doctors, lawyers, accountants, etc. - there are definite differences between those who practice.

One of those differences lies in specialization. By specialization, we mean that a realtor specializes in working within a particular geographic area. As a result, the realtor becomes an expert on how real estate works in that area. They gain a deep, intuitive understanding of things like prices, buildings, and trends. This level of awareness enables the realtor to be of tremendous help to anyone looking for properties in their specific market.

To illustrate the importance of specialization, here's an example. Imagine you wanted to buy a two bedroom, two bathroom condo in downtown Vancouver. One of the realtors you were considering was a specialist in the downtown market. He or she had two decades of experience helping people buy and sell properties there - and only there.

Would you choose this realtor? Or would you choose another, like for instance, a generalist realtor in the Vancouver suburbs? Not exactly a hard choice. The specialist realtor would be your best bet since they'd be far more knowledgeable and capable.

Don't stop at specialization, though. Your realtor should also be someone you can personally get along with. Make sure he/she has a personality that "fits" with your own. Otherwise, the long process of buying a property is going to feel even longer.

To help you determine "fit", I recommend doing interviews. Invite a few prospective realtors to give you their presentations. Then after each presentation, ask the realtor questions and work to get a sense of their personality. Provided that you interview at least a few realtors, you should soon have a clear sense of "fit" and be able to confidently pick one.

Depending on which realtor you choose, you may have to sign a buyer's agreement. This agreement formally commits you to your realtor. Not every realtor requires such an agreement, though. Other realtors will be happy to work with you on faith alone.

Once you select a realtor, the process can begin. Your realtor will probably arrange a meeting to get a sense of what you're looking for in a property. You can expect to answer questions about price and how many bedrooms you need in the property. Your realtor may also ask whether you need various amenities (parking, in-suite laundry), what your time frame is, and what kind of long-term plans you have.

The point of this Q&A is clarity. Your realtor wants to get a sense of what you're after so as to narrow down the search for properties.

Clarity will keep your realtor, for example, from sending you information on a particular two-bedroom condo because it doesn't have in-suite laundry. Conversely, when they find a two-bedroom that does have in-suite laundry, your realtor can then send you the listing - provided that it meets your other criteria too.

Once you have a property that meets your criteria, it's time to physically see it. This is where open houses come in. An open house is an official time in which the person selling a property (or their realtor) allows interested buyers to come and look around. Despite having "house" in their name, open houses are also done for other types of properties. In your case, you might attend an open house for a condo or apartment that you were interested in. Not every property does open houses, though. Depending on which property caught your eye, your realtor might have to make some phone calls and set up a private showing.

As you visit properties, I'd advise you to do more than just look around. You should also be reflecting on the properties from an investor's standpoint. Even though you're buying a place to live in now, you may eventually turn it into an investment property later. So be sure to think as an investor, keeping several items at the forefront of your mind.

First, think about what you can comfortably afford. Of the properties you're looking at, which ones could you buy without using all of your available mortgage? Focus on these "comfortable" properties and, where possible, try to leave yourself a buffer.

If for instance, a bank lets you borrow a maximum of $400,000, don't be ashamed to take out $385,000. There's nothing wrong with leaving yourself a buffer so you're not stretched too thin.

That's easier said than done, however. Depending on how "hot" your city's real estate market is, you may have to go all in on the mortgage. Going all in could be the only way for you to beat out competitors and get the property you want.

If you do have to take out the full mortgage, so be it. But look for an opportunity, where possible, to have a buffer.

Another consideration when looking at properties is location. Actually, it's more like "location, location, location" - as the cliché goes. But the cliché exists because it's true. Location is of paramount importance in real estate.

Location matters in one sense, with where a property is physically located. To illustrate the importance of location in this sense, let's talk about Vancouver.

In my city, I've seen apartments with "scenic" views of the off-ramp to a major bridge. All day and all night, the off-ramp sends cars roaring past the resident's windows.

I've also seen apartments located next to a bus loop. Residents there get to breathe the "savory" fumes from one hundred passing buses every hour.

And, of course, I can't forget the downtown condo that was directly above a twenty-four hour McDonald's. Hopefully the person living there enjoyed the perpetual smell of grease and the constant noise.

Now I can't speak for the owners in these examples, but most of us wouldn't think highly of such addresses. We'd probably prefer different physical locations. And we'd undoubtedly be willing to pay more for those locations. Our willingness therefore demonstrates the way location impacts real estate.

Location is important, but so is price. That's why it can be tempting, for example, to buy a unit located above the entrance to a parking garage. At first glance, this unit might appear to be a steal. The unit could be the same size as others in the building, yet $50,000 less.

Spend any time in the unit, though, and you'll feel the steady vibration of the parking garage gate. Twenty seconds of shaking as the gate opens. And then twenty seconds of shaking as it closes. Again and again, at all hours of the day and night.

No wonder the unit is priced at $50,000 less. A higher price just isn't possible. Not with the parking garage giving you "good vibrations".

Resist the temptation to buy "dog" units like this. For your sanity. And because "dog" units are a terrible long-term investment. In the long run, these kind of units barely appreciate. They're also difficult to rent out and sell. You're far better off, ponying up the money and buying a higher quality unit. As you do, it's natural to think about price. Just make sure you give equal consideration to location - both for the building and for where the unit lies within the building.

Beyond location, a third consideration when looking at properties is rental restrictions. Rental restrictions limit the extent to which condos and apartments in a building can be rented out. Restrictions may be complete (no rentals whatsoever) or partial (some units can be rented).

Rental restrictions matter to us because they threaten our ability to earn passive income. We can't earn passive income from renting out our property if rentals aren't allowed. For this reason, I encourage you to investigate what rental restrictions, if any, exist for properties you're considering. The last thing you want is to buy a unit and then discover later that you can't earn passive income from renting it.

Rental restrictions also matter to those who have no interest in renting out their properties. Suppose, for example, that you buy a property for the sole purpose of living there. In the beginning, rental restrictions probably won't impact you. But imagine that your job or a major life event suddenly compels you to move to another city. In a situation like that, rental restrictions will prevent you from renting out your property. Instead of renting, you'll be forced to sell. As you do, you'll have to settle for whatever the current market conditions are. If it's a strong buyer's market, you may end up taking less money than you'd like or even having a loss.

Suffice to say, then, that you should do your homework when looking at properties. Know what you're getting yourself into, especially with regard to rental restrictions, location, and pricing.

Assuming you actively hunt for properties, you'll eventually find "the one". This will be the condo or apartment that you can see yourself buying. It meets whatever criteria you have and you're sold on it.

When you've found "the one", consult your realtor and have them write an offer. The offer will have the price that you're willing to pay the seller for their property.

"Wait, hasn't the seller already listed their price?"

Yes, but you don't have to accept it. Not immediately anyway. With your realtor's help, you can negotiate to a more favorable price.

As an example, you might see a condo listed at $400,000. You and your realtor would then offer to buy it for $375,000. The condo's seller would counter your offer, asking for $390,000. In response, you'd adjust your offer to $385,000. If the seller accepted this offer, you'd then have the property and for $15,000 less than its original listing price.

Unfortunately, the negotiation process doesn't always go this smoothly. One to two counteroffers from the seller tends to be the standard. Yet depending on the seller, you may have a lengthy back-and-forth negotiation that goes on far, far longer. Or the seller may flatly reject your offer and go with another buyer.

Additionally, the seller could just let the offer "die" on its own. This happens when buyer and seller can't agree on a price. As negotiations break down, the seller lets the offer's allotted time run out. Tomorrow night at 6 PM, for example, comes and goes without any word from the seller. Once this happens, the offer is considered to be "dead".

If your offer dies, don't be discouraged. As long as you keep contacting sellers, you can ultimately succeed in buying your first property.

I'm not just saying that to make you feel good either. Time and again, the people who I see succeeding as buyers are the ones who press on. Even when sellers irritate them. Even when negotiations fall through after a prolonged back-and-forth dialogue. And even in the aftermath, when all the good properties are supposedly taken. Press on and you'll get there, trust me.

You'll officially be "there" when the seller accepts your offer. At this point, the completion of the deal will depend on what specific terms (if any) are in your offer.

If you've made a no subject offer, then there's nothing additional to do. You'd probably make this kind of offer if you were in a bidding war with other buyers. Having no subjects serves to strengthen your offer against the competition.

As an illustration of no subject offers, suppose you're bidding on a property valued at two million dollars. Normally, if you bid $50,000 less than the highest offer, you'd probably lose out on the deal. But imagine that you make a no subject offer and the highest offer you're competing against has multiple subject clauses.

In this latter scenario, your offer now has a fighting chance. You may even win, despite the lower price. Your no subject offer could be the determining factor. A seller would want to avoid delaying the deal while the higher-priced buyer removed subjects from their offer. The seller would rather close now, taking $50,000 less and maintain the selling momentum. Besides, on a two million dollar property, $50,000 barely registers. It's a small sacrifice to avoid the anxiety of waiting for a buyer to remove subjects.

Most buyers - yourself too, perhaps - are making an offer with subjects (conditions). These subjects must be met in order for the deal to go through. In most offers, there are usually three main subjects.

First, the deal is subject to the buyer getting financing locked in. The buyer will already have been pre-approved by their bank or lender for purchasing a property. Now, though, the buyer needs to get their bank/lender to sign off on the specific condo or apartment. This approval on a specific piece of property is essential, or else the buyer may not actually have the ability to pay. So financing needs to get locked in, as one of the main subjects in an offer.

Another of an offer's common subjects is getting all of the condo documents. Condo documents are the records pertaining to the building where an apartment or condo is situated. These documents will have been prepared by the condo or homeowner's association. Condo documents typically include depreciation reports, engineers reports, financials, and two years worth of minutes from previous condo meetings. The point in getting all of these documents is for a buyer to understand the building that they're buying into. If the building's management is financially irresponsible or doesn't respond to owner complaints, the buyer has a right to know this ahead of time. Such issues would likely be apparent from a review of relevant condo documents.

Along with condo documents, a third subject in most offers is getting a home inspection. An inspection would be necessary in order to show the buyer that there were no hidden or overlooked issues in the property. Any issues, if they existed, would be uncovered by a professional home inspector during the inspection. These inspections typically cost about $400 for an attached unit (condo, apartment) and $600 for a house.

If you're buying an attached unit, your inspector will examine such things as heating, appliances, and windows. The inspection is limited, though, because the inspector cannot feasibly inspect the rest of the building. The inspector cannot probe into the building's main power systems, for example, or inspect the units nearby yours. In place of that probing, you'll have to rely on the condo documents and any additional information that you're able to obtain.

If the home inspection doesn't reveal any significant problems with the property, this subject (condition) will be removed from the offer. From there, you'll need to ensure that the other subjects (condo documents and financing) are satisfied, so they can be removed too. Your own offer may also have other subjects too, beyond these three common ones. However many there are, focus on getting the subjects removed. Once you do, your deal can officially close.

At that juncture, a 4% to 5% deposit (in the Vancouver market) will be held in trust with the buying side's brokers. In the context of the deal, the deposit serves as part of the down payment. If, for example, you had a ten percent down payment, then the five percent deposit would equate to roughly half of the down payment. Check with your realtor, though, as the timing of the deposit does vary between jurisdictions.

It's important to realize as well that your deposit is non-refundable. It's non-refundable, so as to show the seller that you're serious about the transaction. The deposit is an expression of good faith, if you will. Hopefully, you really do intend to complete the transaction. But if you don't, the deposit could be in jeopardy and might be forfeited.

Got the subjects removed? Then you've got a firm deal. No more speculation. No more waiting with baited breath. The deal is now legally binding and the deposit is due.

Following this stage, your deal advances toward the completion date. This date is negotiable and specified in the offer. On average, completion comes in another four to six weeks. Some sellers, however, may want a quick closing or a drawn-out one. It just depends.

When the completion date arrives, funds are then transferred between buyer and seller. These funds consist of the following: five percent held as deposit, the rest of the buyer's down payment, and the money from the bank as mortgage.

At the same time, the seller will transfer the title on the property to the buyer. If you're buying, this transfer from the seller officially makes you the new owner of the property.

As you become the new owner, on completion day, the risk on the property officially transfers to you. With the risk, you must now have insurance on the property. Understand this and make sure that your property insurance kicks in on completion day. You may not have the keys to the property yet, but you now own it and are responsible for the property too.

Speaking of getting the keys, that happens the next day. The day after completion. We call "key getting day", the possession date. On possession day, you get the keys and can move into your new property.

Thinking about possession day now, you may feel a bit overwhelmed. After all, look at all the stages we had to go through in order to reach this end point. All of that, just for a single deal.

If you're feeling overwhelmed, I'd advise you to think about activities that previously seemed overwhelming. As a child, the sense of overwhelm probably came when learning to ride a bicycle or tie your shoes. As a young adult, you may have been just as overwhelmed while trying to drive for the first time, or master the basics of the profession you now earn a living in. Yet if you made it through those early moments, you can make it here.

I've got another fascinating lesson for you in the next chapter. We'll be getting into what you do with your new property and how you begin to build your real estate empire.

Four

One property at a time

"Landlords grow rich in their sleep without working,
risking or economizing.

- JOHN STUART MILL, ENGLISH ECONOMIST

■ ■ ■

S top me if you've heard this story before.
It goes something like this...

An average Joe (or Joelle) decides to start a business and become financially independent.

Despite having a full-time job, they begin working on the business.

Months and years of hardship follow.

During this time, our hero/heroine spends most weeknights working alone. No family. No friends. Just the business. And twitchy, sleep-deprived eyes the next morning.

Weekends are even more "fun". While their loved ones are off enjoying life, the aspiring business owner gets to "enjoy" more work. As if 40+ hours at a job and those weeknights weren't enough.

It's hard, no question, but the person manages to push through. Years later, they reach the light at the end of the proverbial tunnel. Arriving at last, they emerge triumphantly with a profitable business and financial independence.

Ever heard that story?

I bet you have.

Maybe in those exact terms, or in some variation.

It's an entertaining story.

One that sells newspapers, books, and keeps shows like "60 Minutes" on the air.

But it's also a misleading story.

Misleading because of what it implies about becoming financially independent.

Hearing the story, you may believe that financial independence is only possible with immense sacrifice. If you want to become independent, you must therefore lead an overworked, sleep-deprived, and socially isolated life. Without that kind of "dedication", you'll never succeed in business and become financially independent. Or so the story goes.

In addition, this story also "teaches" us that a business is the primary vehicle for becoming financially independent. If you want to attain independence, you seemingly must start a restaurant, a store (brick and mortar, or online), a contracting service, or some other type of business.

Both of these "lessons" are wrong, however. Despite what you've heard, the process of becoming financially independent doesn't have to be this hard. You don't have to give up everything you hold dear and become a workaholic. You also don't need to start a business. Not unless you want to.

There's an easier, simpler path. One that allows you to work normal hours, get enough sleep, and maybe (just maybe) have some fun too.

We began walking down this path in the last chapter. That was the chapter where we discussed how to buy your principal residence.

Before we continue on the path, I want to explain why you should buy your principal residence first. Of all the real estate properties you could buy, why this one? Why not cut to the chase, making your first property one that you rent out?

While it's tempting to start with an investment property (i.e, one you rent out), I believe that's a mistake. The reason is that an investment property doesn't give you a roof over your head. It only gives you rent checks from your tenant, which may or may not be enough to cover your housing. Compare that to a principal residence. Own the latter and you won't get a check each month. Instead your principal residence will "pay" you something even more valuable - the peace of mind from knowing you won't be homeless. With that peace of mind, you can relax and focus on your long-term wealth building efforts.

Moving ahead, let's focus now on those long-term efforts. We want to understand what to do once you have your first property. How do you then take that property and use it to advance further down the path toward financial independence?

One option would be to convert your principal residence into a rental property (investment property). This was the approach I took close to three decades ago with my first property.

In my case, I purchased a condo near downtown Vancouver. For eighteen months, the condo was my principal residence. Then, like many adults, I decided to improve my career by going back to school. I began attending community college, taking classes in marketing. My classes were part-time, meaning I could keep my existing job, working for an insurance company.

During this time, I decided to rent out my condo. I put out some ads and succeeded in finding a tenant. The tenant and I subsequently agreed on a monthly rent of $550. For that price, the tenant could live in my condo and I would live elsewhere.

Elsewhere for me, meant my parent's house. My parents allowed me to move back in, provided that I paid them a small monthly rent and continued to hold a full-time job.

Living at home, I could rent out my former principal residence (now an investment property) while still having a roof over my head. The rent that I received went toward paying down the monthly interest payments on the condo. Over the span of five years, the rent payments helped me to make the interest payments, chip away at the principal, and eventually own the condo in full.

My experience with the condo is the reason why I believe converting your principal residence into an investment property might be your next step. Once you've purchased your principal residence, you could follow my lead, changing your principal into an investment property, and looking for a way to rent the property out.

If you make this transition (principal residence to investment property), be sure to adjust your cost base. An adjustment is necessary so you don't end up paying too much in capital gains taxes.

Those taxes won't be an issue while a property is your principal residence. During this time, any increases in the property's value will be considered tax-free capital gains. You won't be required to pay capital gains taxes because the property is your residence. That's great news since your property's value could, for example, increase from $300,000 to $375,000 in just four years. If that happened, you wouldn't pay any taxes on the $75,000 in capital gains, provided that the property remained as your principal residence.

Everything changes, though, when you convert your principal residence into an investment property. Now that the property is no longer your principal residence, you'll be responsible for taxes on capital gains. This is where adjusting your cost base becomes so important.

If you haven't adjusted the cost base, you'll be required to pay taxes on capital gains dating back to when you bought your principal residence. You'll have to pay such far-reaching taxes because there won't be a clear dividing line between the cost base when you first bought the property and the cost base when you converted it. The tax man will have no way of seeing when your capital gains changed from tax-free to taxable. Without clear separation, you'll end up paying capital gains taxes for both your property's principal residence period and its investment property period. This would be unfortunate because capital gains on your principal residence are supposed to be tax-free. It's really one of the main benefits of buying a principle residence in the first place.

Avoid this tragedy by adjusting your cost base right when you convert your property from principal residence to investment property. You can perform the adjustment with the help of a realtor. The realtor will research the values of properties comparable to your own. He or she will also provide a valuation for your property, indicating how much the property costs as of the time it stops being your principal residence. Your responsibility is then to ensure this valuation is formally documented in writing. Get it documented. Then get a third-party appraiser to also document the valuation. This way you'll pay the correct, fair amount of capital gains taxes.

Whatever that amount ends up being, make sure you pay it. All of it. As in the full amount. 100%.

I feel silly having to preach here. Yet it's necessary because some people just don't get it. They seem to believe that tax authorities are simple-minded Amish, who lack the technology and finances to monitor taxpayers. Under this delusion, these people try and cheat on their taxes. Paying less than what is due, or perhaps nothing at all.

The tax authorities, for their part, often do nothing in response. Their lack of action only emboldens the cheaters. A few dollars omitted on the last tax return can then mutate into a few hundred dollars (or more!) omitted on subsequent returns. All the while, cheaters tell themselves that authorities either don't know or don't care.

Until they do.

Suddenly and without warning, the tax man often wakes from his supposed slumber. And then like Rip Van Winkle, he's curious what happened during the long years he was asleep.

I hope that's enough to make the point for you. It should be since this isn't complicated. Just pay your taxes. When they are due. In full. Enough said.

Now, on the subject of converting your property, another point I want to make is that you don't have to move back home. Understand that, even as I advise you to "follow my lead". Moving back home was my approach, but you may not want to do it or even have the option.

No worries there. You can still rent out your principal residence. One way would be to rent a portion of the property.

I did this, for example, with a townhouse twenty years ago. The two-bedroom, two-bathroom townhouse cost $195,000. To acquire it, I put twenty percent down, borrowing $160,000. That equated to a mortgage of about $1,200 per month.

I then found a tenant to rent out the other bedroom and bathroom. With the tenant paying $650, my mortgage was essentially chopped in half. In addition, I was still able to live in the townhouse since only one of the bedrooms was being rented out.

In your case, you might not want to share your residence with someone else. You may wish instead to rent your property out in its entirety and then live elsewhere. If that's how you want to play it, then you'll probably have to buy a second property. A second property gives you somewhere to live while your tenant rents your former principal residence.

Before you buy a second property, I'd encourage you to keep several things in mind.

First, understand that there will never be a "perfect" time to buy property #2. If you're looking to buy a second property and have the money, go for it. Get in the market so that, as we've said, time in the market will beat timing the market.

Along with timing, here's something else to keep in mind. If you're having difficulty getting the money for property #2, you may need to get wildly creative.

Now, when I say get "wildly creative", I'm NOT suggesting you fling yourself off a fiscal cliff and plummet into crushing levels of debt. Don't sign up with ten credit cards, for example, and then max them all out. Don't get entangled with payday loans or "cash on demand" services either. I guarantee that you won't like how things turn out in any of these situations.

When I speak of being creative with financing, I'm suggesting that you look for a way forward using acceptable, above-the-board methods. This is one of the things that I love about real estate as a field. There's almost always a legitimate way forward if you can just think creatively.

Before you get too creative, see what your bank can do for you. Can you tap into some equity on your current property? You may have some money, already in there, which you can just tap into via a home equity line of credit (HELOC) at prime plus a half percent.

If you do have to get creative, you might consider a co-ownership agreement. A co-ownership agreement is one where two parties agree to co-own a property. Co-ownership means that the parties evenly split the down payment, all expenses, and any income from the property. The agreement also enables one of the owners to buy out the other and gain 100% ownership of a property.

A co-ownership agreement can help you get into a second property because it takes some of the financial weight off your shoulders. The agreement puts your name, along with another person's name, on a mortgage and on the title of a property.

Any bank that you approach for the mortgage is now looking at two people and more importantly two incomes, rather than just one. With two people, a bank will feel more comfortable loaning money. That's because if one person defaults on mortgage payments, the bank can attempt to collect these payments from the other person.

For a co-ownership agreement to work, you must have an official written agreement that you and the other party have signed. Oral agreements or email conversations don't count.

You can get the agreement written for you by a lawyer. Expect to spend four to five hundred dollars to have it written. However much the lawyer charges, it's money well spent. That's because you'll be clear on what's expected of you in the agreement, along with what your co-owner's rights and responsibilities are.

Speaking of doing things legally and by the book; you should never attempt to buy your second property with no money down. I mention this idea (no money down) because it's a common ingredient in many "get rich in real estate" schemes. Look around and you'll find numerous infomercials, radio ads, and other media - all advising you to buy with no money down.

Regardless of where you hear the idea, don't fall for it. No money down, as a strategy, doesn't work in any major real estate market. The only people who it does work for are the ones selling courses, books, and other mis-educational content. And for them to make money, you have to lose money.

As you can see, I'm not a fan of no money down. But you don't have to take my word for it. Let's look at the specifics of no money down, to understand what it is and why it's such a fatally flawed premise.

With no money down, the idea is to avoid a down payment by purchasing a property directly from its owner. This is a tantalizing idea because the down payment is usually the biggest hurdle keeping people from buying property. Most people struggle for years to save up enough for their down payment. Yet with a no money down strategy, the down payment ceases to exist. You don't have to make a down payment because you're not dealing with a bank. The bank, which would normally be there to provide you with a mortgage, is nowhere to be seen.

In place of the bank, you're supposed to deal with the owner of a property. Just you and them.

This is where no money down, as a strategy, goes from "that might work" to "you've gotta be kidding". Think about it for a minute and you'll see how ludicrous this whole idea is.

For starters, the property owner needs to have a clear title on the house. In other words, they can't have a mortgage. Any mortgage needs to have been paid off in full. This criteria immediately limits the number of people who could, conceivably, enter into a no money down deal with you.

Then there's the glaring fact that the owner probably wasn't planning on selling their property. The only reason they're considering it now is because you contacted them.

You and the owner are also complete strangers to one another. You've never met before, and probably have little (if anything) in common.

And, of course, there's the unusual circumstances under which you're supposed to reach out to the owner. Can't leave those out. Following the standard no money down script, you'll have made contact with the owner by knocking on their front door.

Knocking on their front door?

Does that sound like a recipe for success in real estate?

Sounds more like a way to get the door slammed in your face. Or physically assaulted by an irate home owner.

No, trying to buy property without any money down just isn't going to work. Even if somehow you did get a deal moving forward, you'd be setting yourself up for numerous problems later on.

You could be sued, for example, with the seller claiming that you withheld information from them during the transaction. The seller could also withhold information from you, never mentioning issues like water damage or liens against the property.

Other problems you could face include being ripped off on price and having to deal with a demanding seller. Additionally, the seller could be so unmotivated that you end up having to do everything - thereby wasting hours of your time.

To avoid all of these problems, steer clear of no money down. It's an ineffective, flawed way of attempting to buy property.

If you want to actually buy property, do it the safe and legal way. With realtors, banks, and lawyers.

Will you have to pay fees to these outside professionals? Most likely. But remember, your goal is to not have to work for money. So if all of your time is eaten up by a lengthy, do-it-yourself real estate transaction, you're not getting ahead.

You're also not getting ahead by selling your own home. Doing a "FSBO" (for sale by owner) is another counterproductive idea that runs in the same delusional do-it-yourself spirit as no money down. "FSBO"s commonly appeal to those who wish to avoid paying commissions to realtors.

"Wait, aren't you a realtor?"

Yes, and I receive a commission when people sell their homes. I'm not going lie to you about that.

But I'm not receiving a commission for giving you practical advice on real estate in this book. So if I can speak freely, let me advise you again to not try selling your own property.

The "FSBO" approach should be avoided because it underexposes your property. If you take this track, you're voluntarily limiting the number of offers you can receive. You won't be getting many offers because your property lacks visibility on the market.

Visibility wouldn't be a problem if you were using a realtor. With a realtor, your property would be visible to thousands of people on the multiple listings service (MLS). Anyone who was interested could then contact you and make an offer. Given the size of the MLS, you might soon end up with several appealing offers.

That's if you were using a realtor.

But as a "FSBO", you're not using a realtor. So you can't post to the MLS. You've got to rely instead on methods like posting a "For Sale" sign outside your home and asking your friends if they know anyone who wants to buy. You'll also probably be posting it on Craigslist, and with that alone - who knows the kind of potential buyers you'll attract?

Is it any wonder that "FSBO"s have to settle for whatever they can get?

The lack of visibility causes there to be so few offers that a "FSBO" seller is desperate to accept any buyer.

If, on the other hand, you enlist a realtor to sell your property, you won't have to settle for whatever you can get. Your realtor can put your property on the MLS, instantly increasing its chances of being seen.

Additionally, your realtor may also put out a "cooperating commission" - which incentivizes other realtors to find a buyer. When I do this, for example, I'll offer a $7,500 cooperating commission on a $500,000 condo and pay it to any realtor who brings me and my client a buyer. This commission typically leads to a flood of offers, as other realtors now have a reason to send me prospective buyers.

I've drifted here, talking about "FSBO"s. The last thing I'll say on this, is that you shouldn't fixate on realtor commissions.

In place of commissions, think about what you'll net from the deal. The net amount is how much goes in your bank account after your property is sold. It's what matters at the end of the day. To you anyway.

As an example of net, suppose you sold a property as a "FSBO" for $900,000. In this case, you'd net $900,000 and pay nothing to a realtor.

Not bad, right? Maybe, but how do you know you got a good price? If you exposed your property to the market, with a realtor's help, you could probably net even more. In our example here, a realtor might be able to sell your property for one million dollars. If the deal worked out, the realtor might then take $30,000 as total commission. Of that commission, the listing realtor would take half ($15,000) and the buying realtor would get the other $15,000.

You'd be left with $970,000 net. That means you'd make $70,000 more, working with a realtor versus doing a "FSBO". And the realtor would handle the sale for you, meaning far less work than with a "FSBO" too.

More money and less work? That's what you can expect when you work with a realtor. You're also unlikely to get sued, since a realtor will draft a legally binding contract for the deal.

Knowing all this, I'd encourage you once more to avoid fixating on realtor commissions. The commission is ultimately a trivial sum compared to what you gain - whether that's net or just peace of mind.

Getting back on track, let's focus now on renting out your first property. We've just covered what you need to know so you can buy a second property and move into it. With the first property vacant, it's time to begin renting it.

So, what do you do?

You find a tenant. That's the first step in renting your property. Find a tenant so you can have someone paying you rent.

With the advent of the internet, finding a tenant has never been easier. There are countless online channels to use for this. My personal favourite is Craigslist. When I need to rent a property, I'll post an ad on Craigslist and then wait for the phone to ring.

This is a far cry from how things were fifteen to twenty years ago. At that time, I'd spend $125 for a forty word classified ad. The ad would run in Vancouver's two biggest newspapers for three days (Thursday, Friday, Saturday) and I'd hopefully get some phone calls about it. Now, with Craigslist, the advertising is free and lasts much longer than three days. And, most importantly, it works. A recent ad that I ran, for example, led to fifteen calls in four hours. From there, I was able to book seven showings of the property the very next day.

Along with Craigslist, you could also try to find a tenant using the website Airbnb (Airbnb.com). Airbnb is a site that allows anyone to rent out rooms, apartments, houses, or other property. Originally, Airbnb served as a means of finding a place to stay while traveling. Recently, however, many people have begun using the site to find long-term living arrangements. So many people are apparently using the site in this way that Airbnb has changed their branding. The site's tagline is now "Welcome Home" and its logo is a paperclip-like image that represents "belonging". Both of these changes reflect the new reality of Airbnb as a platform for finding housing.

While you could use Airbnb to find your tenant, I'd personally advise against it. My rationale is that using Airbnb to find a tenant can put you at odds with your condo's regulations. These regulations, created by the homeowner's association, usually state that the minimum rental period for condo units is six months. Most homeowner's associations do this to keep their condo complexes from becoming hotels. Yet Airbnb, even with its rebranding, is still about short-term, often night-to-night rentals. This means that you're unlikely to find a tenant wishing to rent for six months or more using Airbnb. You might. But it's far more likely that your Airbnb listing will attract short-term renters.

If you were then to take those renters, you'd be violating the rules of the homeowner's association. The homeowner's association might never find out, but why take that chance? Do you really want to build your long-term real estate portfolio on such shaky ground? I wouldn't recommend it. You're playing with fire and it's completely unnecessary. There are enough other platforms out there to use in finding tenants.

While I don't recommend using Airbnb to find tenants, I do believe the website can be useful. Airbnb might be of great use to you, if you don't mind essentially running a hotel. In that case, you could earn a respectable income off nightly rentals. People would rent your Airbnb space, just like they would with a regular hotel room. And you'd get to charge them regular hotel room prices.

I can't speak for hotel rates in your location. But I do know that in downtown Vancouver, where I'm situated, those rates start at $150 per night. Also, Airbnb's average nightly stay tends to be about two to three nights. So if about ten people booked your property each month - for twenty nights total - you'd earn $3,000 every month. That's 50% more than the monthly rent on a typical one bedroom condo in the same part of Vancouver. Your 50% extra comes with much more work. But if you're willing to do it - and your homeowner's association approves - knock yourself out!

Airbnb is also useful for those of us who do traditional, long-term property rentals. Here, the website is re-shaping the market in our favor. Airbnb is doing this by enticing other property owners to convert their vacant, unfurnished units into furnished, hotel-like properties. This reduces the number of options that long-term tenants have for housing. With less housing available, rent prices go up. We, as property owners, can thus charge higher rents each month. All thanks to Airbnb.

Setting Airbnb aside, concentrate on platforms like Craigslist. Doing that, you should have no difficulty attracting interested tenants. What might be difficult for you is separating the "good" tenants from the "bad" ones. Sadly, there's no "silver bullet" to determine the quality of a tenant. What you can do, though, is look at a few tried-and-true items.

First, look at when the prospect is contacting you. Are they contacting you a month or more before your property will be available to rent? If so, this suggests that you're dealing with someone who takes initiative and doesn't procrastinate. A prospective tenant of this sort will probably begin looking for their next place at least one month in advance. Prospects like this would, for example, be visiting properties at the end of May to move in on July 1st. Look for these proactive prospects in the last six days of a month.

In that period, the ideal renter will have given their current landlord one month's notice of their intent to move out. With the notice delivered, this type of renter is eager to visit your property and potentially agree to renting it. The last couple days of a given month and the first four or five days of the next month, are therefore when the "magic" of finding your tenant usually occurs.

All the same, not every prospective tenant is going to be working well in advance of dates and deadlines. I see this with some of my tenants, for example, when they move out. My tenants are required to provide at least thirty days notice to vacate. Yet sometimes these tenants find a new rental right as they vacate the old one.

Is this due to procrastination? Perhaps. But even if these tenants are procrastinating, it doesn't necessarily make them bad prospects. That's why I believe it's important to place timing in context, alongside other considerations.

Another of those considerations is how a prospective tenant dresses and behaves. When you meet them, is the prospect wearing pants so loose that they spend more time trying to stay clothed than talking to you? That could be a bad sign. I'm no fashion critic, though, so don't immediately rule someone out on dress alone.

The same goes for prospective tenants who are late to a showing. Maybe they really did get a flat tire after driving their sick grandmother to the hospital. These things do happen. Rarely. But it's always a possibility.

What you're doing with all these considerations, is building a mental database. Each consideration is like a piece of data in that database. Once you have enough data, you'll be able to predict future behavior from a prospective tenant.

You'll have a chance to build that database when showing prospective tenants your property. Showing a property is the next step after you've advertised it. For a showing, you'll meet with a prospect for about ten to fifteen minutes. During this time, you give them a tour of the available rental and answer any questions they have. Then, at the end, you provide the prospect with an "Application for Tenancy".

This application is a piece of paper asking for personal information from the prospective tenant. Information on the application usually includes: the prospect's name, their social security number, their driver's license number, their current employer, and contact details for their current landlord. An ideal "Application for Tenancy" will also ask for references, who are not related to the prospect.

After you give a prospective tenant the "Application for Tenancy", the onus is on them. If they're interested in the property, the prospect will complete the application and send it back to you. They must take this action in order to move beyond talk. For talk, as the saying goes, is cheap. Too cheap to afford your rent. And too cheap to be of any use, beyond giving you a temporarily burst of hope.

If you do get an application back, then it's your turn once more. Your next step should be to run a credit check on the prospective tenant. I say "should" because you don't technically have to take this step. But there's no reason not to. A credit check, using an online service like Equifax only takes ten minutes. You'll have to spend some time initially, signing up for the credit check service. But once the sign-up is complete, ten minutes is all it takes to run the credit check. In that time, you'll learn the real story about a prospective tenant's finances. Do they really have good credit? Or were they lying to you? A credit check doesn't lie, so you'll get the truth.

Assuming you use Equifax, the truth comes as a "Beacon Score". This score is a number on a scale from zero to nine-hundred. On this scale, a favorable score will generally be above six hundred. Anything under six hundred indicates that your prospect has "poor" credit. Renting to someone with a sub-six hundred beacon score would therefore be a major mistake.

Keep in mind that the ranges I've just given you, for beacon scores, can vary depending on your market. In my case, many of the people I deal with are high-income professionals. For this kind of market, it's reasonable for me to expect scores to be at least in the high six hundred's or mid seven hundred's. Most of the people I've rented to lately are even higher than that too, with beacon scores up in the eight hundred's. For other markets, though, these ranges may need to be adjusted a bit. If you're renting to a working-class market, you probably shouldn't expect your prospects to all have beacon scores of eight hundred or more. Know the context and adjust your standards accordingly.

If the credit check shows your prospective tenant has a good credit history, you should then check their references. Make a few quick phone calls to the prospect's employer, their previous landlord, and other people they listed on the rental application. As with the credit check, calling references may take some time, yet it will save you massive headaches later on.

Tenant-related headaches are worth avoiding for two reasons. First, it's just plain annoying having to deal with various issues caused by your tenants. You've got better things to do with your time than chase a tenant for the rent or get them to stop playing loud music at 2 AM.

Also, headaches from your tenants will, over time, burn you out. You'll probably come to feel that all tenants are annoying and not worth dealing with. Bad experiences with tenants usually leave this kind of sour taste in your mouth. If you have enough of them, you won't want to rent to anyone. This is overwhelmingly the number one reason I get calls from owners wishing to sell their investment properties. They just can't take it anymore. And that's precisely why it's important to properly screen prospective tenants. You don't want bad tenants to burn you out, resulting in anxiety now and absolute heartache when you take yourself out of the market later and watch in horror as your property appreciates spectacularly without you.

As you do your screenings, don't panic if your rental sits empty. I know it's hard to believe, but there are worse things in life than losing a month's rent. One of those "worse things" would be having a deadbeat tenant who trashes your condo and doesn't pay rent. Someone you accepted as a renter out of desperation.

If you haven't found the right tenant yet, wait. As with dating, there are plenty of fish in the sea. "Mr./Ms. Right" is out there. Your property just hasn't met them yet. Give it some time, continue advertising, and you're bound to get an ideal renter.

I'm confident that you can find the right person to rent because not all tenants are monsters. Most are actually normal and level-headed. And if you price your unit properly, doing sufficient due diligence, you'll have no trouble finding them.

When at last you do find that "perfect" tenant, they'll need to sign a tenancy agreement. This agreement is available online from providers like Self-Council Press (http://www.self-counsel.com/). The tenancy agreement will include the start and end date of tenancy, along with rental conditions like no smoking. Tenancy agreements also require tenants to read and acknowledge receipt of the by-laws and regulations for the building where they're renting.

And, tenants must include a security deposit with the tenancy agreement. In British Columbia, where I work, the deposit is equal to one-half of the month's rent. Depending on where you live, the deposit may be greater than or equal to this amount.

The deposit protects you against damages the tenant may cause to your condo. Hopefully, though, you've found a tenant who's not going to damage the condo. If they leave the place intact, the deposit will be fully refundable at move out.

Along with damages, the deposit can also protect you from financial surprises. I avoid those surprises by always getting a deposit check from incoming tenants, weeks before they move in. I'll then cash the check immediately, to make sure the tenant is good for the money. If, or most likely when, the deposit check clears; I'll have the deposit and one more reason to feel optimistic about my incoming tenant.

The deposit and the tenancy agreement go hand-in-hand with another document, Form K. This document contains the tenant's emergency contact information. Building management needs this information so they'll know who to contact if there's ever a problem in the unit. If management ever smells smoke, for example, they may want to give the tenant a call and make sure everything's alright in the condo. Having Form K allows them to do so.

A third form that your tenant will need to sign is an inspection checklist. This is a list of all the items in the unit and the condition of each at move-in. Common items on the checklist include the condition of the carpeting and whether appliances in the unit work. As a best practice, you should do this inspection with the tenant when they move in. Walk through the unit with them and make sure you're on the same page now about any irregularities in the condo. If for instance, the tiles in the bathroom are cracked; this needs to be noted in the inspection checklist. Otherwise, you and the tenant may disagree later, on when the tiles cracked.

After a tenant has completed all of these forms, you'll need to collect the first month's rent from them. I personally do this by asking for a currently-dated check, along with eleven post-dated checks. The currently-dated check (i.e. a regular check) goes toward rent in the initial month. The remaining checks, all post-dated, are then cashed one month at a time as rent becomes due. Having these post-dated checks keeps me from having to chase a tenant for a physical check each month. Using the post-dated check for a given month, all I have to do is go to the bank and cash it.

I'm old-school, though. A lot of landlords who are more tech-savvy use an automatic deposit. They get tenants permission to have the payments automatically deposited into an account by electronic transfer.

With the first month's rent in hand, you can then give your tenant the key to the condo. This should not, however, be the last time you speak to the tenant. Stay in contact with the tenant for as long as they rent. This ensures the tenant is satisfied and will, most likely, continue renting.

If staying in contact sounds like a lot of work, just imagine how annoying it will be to go about finding a new tenant. You'll have to jump again through all of the same hoops we just covered. Unless you enjoy that process and all of the paperwork, you're probably not eager to continually find new tenants. This is why it's important to keep in contact with your tenant(s) on a regular basis.

You also want to be responsive when tenants contact you. Most often, they'll reach out to inform you of a problem. Maybe it's a broken appliance, like the dishwasher for example. Or, the problem might be more serious than that. Water might be leaking into the tenant's bedroom from an unknown source above. This actually happened to me in one of my rental units a few years ago. It's a long story, but I can tell you that it involved shots of tequila and an ill-advised shower.

When your tenant calls you about water leaks or their broken dishwasher, you need to act. Fast. Get the problem resolved right away. This kind of response shows tenants that you care. And if your tenants believe, rightfully so, that you care; they'll have one less reason to move out.

You can also keep tenants satisfied by not raising their rents. I'd advise leaving rents alone for two to four years. There's no reason to raise the rent during this time, as long as your tenant behaves and keeps the rental unit in good condition. Raising the rent will only agitate the tenant and give them a reason to consider leaving. And if the tenant leaves, you'll no longer have their rent coming in, as a source of monthly passive income.

Besides, you can't legally raise the rent by that much anyway. About two to three percent if you absolutely wanted to. Are a few dollars of extra rent money worth jeopardizing your passive income? Probably not.

Not in the long-term game you're playing. With that investor's mindset from Chapter Two. Remember, the investor doesn't chase small money. And an extra $20 in rent money is just that. Small money. In place of the small money, an investor focuses on long-term, money-making opportunities. They would look at your tenant, for example, and see a multi-year asset. The kind of asset that, if nurtured and cared for, will produce consistent passive income.

I'm not saying you should only see you tenant as a paycheck. He or she is a human being, after all. My point is only to highlight how important your tenant is to your own passive income and financial independence.

That's really what this is all about. Creating passive income and using it to become financially independent.

The process we've highlighted in this chapter will put you on that path. Given all of the material and numerous tangents; let's review what the process entails.

Quite simply, you buy your principal residence and live in it for a period of time. Then, when you can afford it, you buy a second place to live. With the next place, you no longer have to live in your first property. The first property can then be rented out to a tenant who you've carefully screened.

The tenant pays you rent on the property each month. With each rent payment, you pay down the mortgage, monthly maintenance costs, property taxes. You'll also need to set aside some money for occasional repairs. The carpet will wear out, for example. Or the dishwasher will go. Expect these repairs, they happen.

Any money that's left after paying all those expenses becomes profit for you.

Over time, as the mortgage is steadily paid off, the amount you have left over in profit increases. Eventually, the mortgage is fully paid; leaving you with just monthly maintenance fees and expenses (taxes, unforeseen repairs) each month. At this point, you're making a healthy passive income flow from rent paid for your initial property. The rent continues coming in each month because you respect your tenant and treat them like gold. With your former principal residence (now an investment property) producing passive income, you're ready to "rinse and repeat" the process. Calling up your realtor, you begin the hunt for property #3...

That's the process. As you can see, it doesn't require working nights and weekends. Nor does this process require sacrificing your social life. You can continue to lead your life in much the same way.

The only changes you'll have to make are with respect to mindset and knowledge. On mindset, you'll need to begin thinking like an investor. That means, as we've said, avoiding pick-up games of "small ball" to focus on the long-term.

As for knowledge, you'll need to get "hungry" for useful information on real estate and finance. Become a student in these areas, constantly looking for reputable sources to learn from.

This book is intended as one source of knowledge. Reading it now, you're getting all of the knowledge I've accumulated over my years in real estate.

In the next chapter, you'll be getting even more of that knowledge. I'm going to let you in on some secrets about what it takes to succeed as a real estate investor.

This is material I've never shared with anyone. You won't find it on my "Inside Edge" video blog or in any other formats. I've held these secrets close for years, using them to thrive in the highly competitive Vancouver real estate market. With this book, though, I'm willing to open up. I'm at the stage in my career, where I'm ready to help younger generations get into real estate. Sharing some of my best secrets about real estate investing is one way to do that.

The first secret I'd like to share with you is something I call "The Ghost Ship to Wealth" When you're ready, turn the page and see how you can take your real estate "game" to the next level.

"A Ghost Ship to Wealth"

What is it about money? Everyone seems to want it. But hardly anyone wants to openly talk about it.

People rarely share, for example, how much money they make or how exactly they make it.

On one hand, you can't blame them. Those who talk too much about money are often seen as greedy. There's also a fear of driving others to jealousy or becoming a target for theft.

Yet those aren't the only reasons many people refuse to openly talk about money. Their refusal often comes from an added fear of the unknown. A fear of what tomorrow holds financially.

Tomorrow, or twenty years from tomorrow; you might have nothing in your bank account. No money whatsoever. Or you might barely be making ends meet. Either is a scary thought. One the average person avoids thinking about, and certainly won't willingly bring up in conversation.

The irony is that such refusals can actually be what causes financial failure. As the saying goes, "what you resist will persist". So if you're concerned about your financial future, avoiding talk or thoughts of money will only make it worse.

The only way to resolve your concerns is to face them. Get money out in the open. Think carefully on money. And have whatever conversations are required to secure your financial future.

Nice pitch, huh? Sounds like a set-up to buy financial services. But it's not. I'm not a financial adviser. In fact, I'm quite skeptical about many of them. I'm also not trying to sell you any financial services or products. You won't find me peddling anything like that.

Instead, my true motive is to reinforce for you, the importance of securing tomorrow's finances today. Of all the ways you can do that, I believe real estate ranks among the absolute best.

With real estate, you can secure your financial future through what I call the "ghost ship principal". This is the idea that investment in real estate gives you a "ship" on which to sail toward a strong financial future. You're the captain of this ship, overseeing its direction. Absent from your ship, however, is a crew to sail it. Your ship sails instead by itself. As though ghosts were at the helm.

Like a spirit, your ghost ship is "damned". Damned to sail onward forever. Through night and day. Through calm waters and the stormiest of seas. Never stopping for a moment.

"Damned" too, in the sense of being a damned good investment! Remember we're talking about investing in real estate. And in that context, what better investment than one which is permanently moving ahead, on autopilot, with minimal effort on your part? We may describe it with ghost images, but there's nothing ghastly about the results. This kind of investment will delight you in securing your financial future.

Let's zoom in a bit now. Getting specific on what the investment is that you're making with the "ghost ship principal". By "investing", we mean buying an investment property and then holding it for twenty-five years.

You acquire the investment initially, by purchasing a condo or other real estate property. A down payment is required for this, so it can take you some time to save. But once you do get the money for the down payment, you can buy your property.

From there, you rent the property out to a tenant, following the procedure I've outlined earlier in this book. Your tenant pays rent which becomes your income from the property. You then apply this rental income toward paying off your mortgage and most of your expenses on the property. Eventually, the mortgage is paid off and the rent begins to cover all the property's expenses each month, while leaving you a profit.

At this point, you have a cash-producing vehicle that's also - since it's real estate - steadily appreciating in value. You can sell the asset, realizing a gain since it was purchased. Or you can sit back, content to collect checks indefinitely (or in ghost terms - till Judgment Day).

And all from one investment. A single one. That's all it takes to set your ghost ship out to sea. The hardest part is really just getting that down payment. Saving the money to put a down payment on your first property and buy it. If you can only do that, you'll set yourself up for incredible gains 20 or 30 years later. Yet it's hard.

I personally remember working multiple jobs to raise the money for my down payment. I worked as a hotel doorman, a dishwasher, and a construction worker. Doing work that was often seemingly "beneath" me. Fortunately, I never saw it that way.

I looked at such jobs like Bill Gates does in his famous "11 Rules of Life" speech. In his speech, Gates remarks that "your grandparents had a different word for burger flipping. They called it opportunity".

Opportunity. Yes, opportunity. That's how I saw my jobs to get the money for a down payment. And it's how I believe you must see similar work. You don't necessarily need to do low-wage, part-time jobs. But if that's what it takes, seize the opportunity. Don't sit on the sidelines because you're "too good" to roll up your sleeves and work. Get working! The sooner you do, the sooner you'll have the down payment and can put your ghost ship in motion.

No more sermons, though. Let's look beyond my preaching. At what I've practiced. We'll do that with 33 W. Pender Street, Vancouver BC. It's an investment unit that reflects the "ghost ship principal". Looking at 33 W. Pender Street, you can see what it actually takes to set a ghost ship out to sail.

In this example, I represented the buyer of a one-bedroom, one-bathroom condo. At the time (April 2016), we'd been in competition for the unit with two other parties. The competition saw it as a great buy too, and they wanted in. So we had to make an offer above the condo's asking price ($429,000) in order to acquire it. Our winning offer ended up being $450,000.

To get the down payment, my client (the new owner) needed to put down 20%. He did so as an investor, planning to rent the property and hold it for the long term. Had he been buying a principal residence, however, the unit could be purchased with as little as 5% down. (As a reference - The percent down depends on the purchase and the buyer's own financial qualifications.)

For his 20% down, my buyer got six-hundred and seventy-one square feet of opportunity. Plus a small balcony and a parking space. Seizing the opportunity, he posted his new unit on Craigslist. Within a short time, a tenant came forward willing rent the place for $2,100 per month. The tenant would rent on a one-year lease, and go month-to-month afterward.

Their rent translates into an annual income of $25,200 for the unit's owner (i.e. the buyer).

It's a nice income, but the owner won't see much of it initially. They still have to pay off the mortgage every month. With 20% down to buy the property ($90,000), the remaining total mortgage is $360,000. It's on a 25-year amortization and locked in a three-year term at 2.2%. Meaning the condo's new owner is responsible for monthly mortgage payments of approximately $1,561.17.

Since it's an investment unit, the owner can only deduct the interest from their rental income. In year one, the total interest is $7,810.28. By comparison, the total principal is $10,923.76. Together that amounts to $18,732 in total mortgage due (interest + principal) for year one.

Curious what the interest and principal would be for you? If, or better yet when, you invest in a property. You can get the scoop on interest and principal in your own case by visiting Calculator.net. The site offers a mortgage calculator. It's a great resource for determining the annual amortization table on the full twenty-five years of a mortgage.

With the calculator, you can see how much of your monthly mortgage payment would go towards principal and how much would go towards interest. (For more on this, see the example in Chapter 3)

Returning to Pender Street, let's now look at the buyer's expenses. One of those expenses is a monthly condo maintenance fee of $371.92. Times twelve months in a year. Making $4,463.04 in annual condo maintenance fees.

The buyer also needs to pay property taxes ($1,247.98) and an additional $100 per month ($1,200 annually), for additional repairs that might be necessary. With the total mortgage payment mentioned before ($18,732), the buyer's total expenses for year one are $25,643.02.

Now recall the annual income from renting the unit, $25,200. The buyer deducts their expenses from this rental income. Doing the math ($25,200 - $25,643.02), they are thus left with a loss of about $442 for year one.

A loss? Yes, but not a huge one. And fear not. For year one is the "eye" of the interest "hurricane". The spot where it's most intense. Every year after, the interest payment will gradually decrease. So for the buyer, their "take-home amount" (rental income minus expenses) will increase every year, beyond any rent increase.

If you're having difficulty seeing how this works, here's the math in simple terms. What follows are two basic calculations that put all the pieces together.

Calculation #1

First, we see what the income would be on the Pender Street property.

To arrive at that figure, we take the total rental income minus the expenses you can deduct. Those deductible expenses are interest on the mortgage, condo maintenance fees, taxes, and miscellaneous expenses.

Here's what it looks like mathematically –

Annual expenses on unit:

Interest on mortgage:	$7,810.28	
Condo maintenance fee:	$4,463.04	($371.92 per month x 12 months/year)
Property tax:	$1,247.98	
Allowance for repairs:	$1,200.00	(estimated $100 per month x 12 months/year)

Total annual expenses on unit: $14,721.30 (Sum of 4 totals above)

Annual income from unit

Total rental income:	$25,200.00	
Total expenses for year:	$14,721.30	

Total annual income from unit: $10,478.70 (Difference between 2 totals above)

As you look at these totals, realize that the $10,478.70 is profit. As profit, it will be added to your annual income and taxed at your marginal tax rate. So with 20%, you're earning income on the property. Your income will then increase every year beyond any rent increase because the interest payment each year will decrease.

Calculation #2

Our second calculation is from a cash-flow basis. When we examine Pender Street in this way, it's close to break-even.

Here's why, again in mathematical terms –

Total expenses:

Total mortgage payment:	$18,732.00	(interest + principal =$1,561.17 x 12 mo/year)	
Total on all other fixed costs:	$6,911.02	(condo maintenance fee:	$4,463.04
		+ Property tax:	$1,247.98
		+ Repairs allowance:	$1,200.00)
Total expenses:	$25,643.02	(Sum of 2 totals above)	

Cash Flow

Total expenses:	$25,643.02	
Total rental income:	$25,200.00	
Total cash flow:	-$443.02	(Difference of 2 totals above)

No, the little dash you see next to cash flow (above) isn't a typo. It really does indicate a negative cash flow on Pender Street. So the owner will be supplementing the rental income by approximately $443.02 per year, or $37 per month. They'll be paying this supplement in order to cover the cost of the full mortgage payment (principal + interest), plus all other expenses.

A final point on our calculations is that the $100/month for miscellaneous repairs is not mandatory. It may not actually be needed. We've used it here for the sake of our example.

Also, the repairs amount may not necessarily be $100/month ($1,200/annually). I've leaned on the conservative side with that number. It reflects my personal tendency to leave $1,200 to $1,500 annually as a buffer to cover unexpected repairs or special levies from the Strata. Yet an owner could go five or ten years without spending an extra dime above his monthly condo maintenance fees.

Do you want to chance it? Maybe. But again, I like to lean on the more conservative side. And I think it's wise for a landlord to do the same - always setting aside a bit of extra money each month for unexpected emergencies.

How are you feeling now with those calculations? Do they make our example clearer for you? Hopefully they do. But if you're still lost, don't worry. Feel free to post your questions or comments on my YouTube blog at www.youtube.com/owenbigland. And be sure to subscribe to my YouTube video blog to get notified of my weekly updates.

Now, in discussion of Pender Street, another thing to realize is that you're creating wealth in two ways. First, you're paying down the principal each year. And then second, you're tapping into capital gains via price appreciation.

You really just need to, as my buyer did, put down that $90,000 (or whatever your down payment is). Once that's done and you acquire a property, you'll have a simple wealth generating machine on auto-pilot. The unit that you acquire will then double in the next fifteen to eighteen years. I'm being ultra-conservative here too. Since condos have been doubling in less than ten years lately. Still, look at least fifteen to eighteen years in the future - if for no other reason than to maintain your long-term investor's mindset. On that time frame, you'll end up with a one million dollar asset and very little money left on the mortgage. It'll be a wealth machine, set in motion with a simple $90,000 purchase. You set it, hold the asset, and forget about it.

Get the picture? It's happening on 33 Pender Street. And it's waiting to happen for you.

As you look to build your "wealth machine", that "ghost ship" - you may be tempted to avoid cities like Vancouver. Your rationale might be the low cap rate on investments in real estate.

Then again, "cap rate" might be a completely foreign word for you. Either way, let's discuss it. So we're clear.

To review, a simple cap rate calculation determines the net operating income, or the net income realized by the owner. All operating expenses are subtracted, but not the mortgage. So, for this calculation we're valuing the property as if you paid cash for it.

The "issue" with cap rates is that when buying an investment property in a hot real estate city like Vancouver, your cap rate is not going to be that impressive.

At 33 Pender Street, for example, you'd start on cap rate by looking at your annual rental income of $25,200. Next, you'd deduct monthly condo maintenance, property taxes, and general repairs. Those collectively total $6,911. With the deduction, your total net operating income is $18,289.

Net operating income ($18,289) gets divided by the purchase price of the unit ($450,000). The result is a cap rate for the property of .0406 or just 4%.

Having 4% as your cap rate is not exactly exciting and many investors may feel it's too low. That's why you may consider looking elsewhere. Surely you can do better in other markets.

Here's where you're right, in part. I acknowledge, for example, that in places like Houston, Texas and other mid-Western U.S. cities; you can indeed generate a much better cap rate. In those markets, you might buy a large detached home for $450,000 and then rent it out for $3,000 month. Now there's a cap rate worth celebrating. A whopping 8%!

Still, before popping the champagne, keep in mind the appreciation. This is the capital gain potential on a property over the next fifteen to twenty years. In most of these mid-Western cities, the capital gain is much lower than what you would get in Vancouver. And capital gains matter. They're more favourable to the long-term investor because they are taxed at a much lower rate than income.

So, from a long-term perspective, I still recommended setting your real estate sights on cities like Vancouver - regardless of the lower cap rates. It's a better overall play for you. And better for your ghost ship too, since it sets the ship on course for brighter financial horizons.

Five

Thinking like an investor

"If you can't purchase and be able to hold a property
for at least 8 to 10 years, then you have no business
investing in Real Estate."

- Owen Bigland

■ ■ ■

This book isn't your first exposure to real estate principles.
Believe it or not.

You probably heard one of real estate's most important ideas years ago. Long before you ever picked up this book. Think back on your childhood and you'll see what I mean.

As a child, you were probably taught to be patient. I can't say who gave you this lesson. You might have learned it from your parents, your elementary school teachers, a religious figure, or someone entirely different. But whoever it was, they advised you on the importance of patience. Patience was said to be a virtue. Something to aspire towards.

Funny how things change. Flash forward to the present, and patience often seems like a lost cause. I'm not saying you're necessarily impatient today. But it's harder, isn't it? Harder to do as you were told in childhood and exercise patience.

As adults, we often eschew patience in favor of instant gratification. This can be as simple as ordering fast food, when we lack the patience to cook healthy food. Or, it can be more complex - as when we're impatient toward investments.

It's in this latter case that real estate enters the picture. When investing in real estate, patience is definitely a virtue. If you can only heed the advice you were given years ago - to be patient - you can invest and attain success in real estate.

The problem, though, is that many aspiring real estate investors lack patience. To them, patience is for kids. These impatient investors want their gains now, not in a decade or two.

Maybe they need to go back to elementary school. That might remind these investors that patience is still a virtue.

I say this jokingly since the only adult who can plausibly return to elementary school is Adam Sandler (in the comedy Billy Madison). What isn't a joke are the consequences of a lack of patience. If you can't patiently invest in real estate, you're unlikely to ever achieve financial independence. Instead, you're likely to end up frustrated, financially worse off, and convinced that success in real estate is unattainable.

I don't want you to end up in that position. You probably don't want that either. So let's take a moment now to understand what it means to lack patience in real estate. This is the number one reason I see real estate investors fail. And it's more complex than you'd expect. In general, there are three primary ways in which real estate investors demonstrate a lack of patience. Understand these ways and you can keep yourself from behaving in a similarly self-sabotaging manner.

The first way I see aspiring investors lack patience is when looking at market fluctuations.

The simple truth is that markets fluctuate. They go up for a while. Then they go down, taking a breather. They stay flat, often treading water for years. And then the markets go up once more, repeating this dance. It's a fact of life. Something so simple an elementary school student could understand. And to their credit, most aspiring investors understand the "dance" of the markets. It's just not a "dance" they're comfortable with.

Despite knowing in their head that the markets will recover, many aspiring investors still feel nauseous whenever fluctuations occur. The motions of the market leave them wanting to throw up their properties - on the MLS that is - and cash out ASAP.

When aspiring investors behave like this, it indicates a lack of patience. If these wannabe investors would only be patient, they'd see the market rise again. The market's recovery probably wouldn't come overnight. But it would happen. Eventually.

This is the reason I've advised you in the past to buy and hold properties for at least eight to ten years. Holding for that length of time (or longer) gives you enough runway to ride out short-term volatility in the market. When the volatility comes, continue holding on to your property/properties. Be patient, knowing that market fluctuations are just par for the course.

Can you do that?

You need to, in order to make real money. Whether we're talking real estate or other investment areas like stocks; your success is directly tied to your ability to be patient amid market fluctuations.

If you can't do that, you'll have to settle for seemingly safe, non-market-driven approaches. It appears safe, for example, to put your money in a bank account. The bank probably isn't going anywhere and only you can withdraw the money.

But consider what you're missing out on here. You're losing money due to inflation. And you're also losing out on the chance for strong returns, over time, as a result of being involved in a market. Over time, such returns would enable you to build wealth and financial security. The same cannot be said for any returns you'd get from a bank account.

Your bank account, for example, is never going to give you a one hundred percent return. But in real estate? Well that's another story. On a real estate investment, it's hardly a stretch to envision getting a return of one hundred percent. Depending on the investment, you might find that your real estate returns an even higher percentage too.

You just need patience. That's the only way you'll be able to invest in a real estate market and avoid queasiness when the market inevitably fluctuates. With patience, you can be comfortable during the fluctuations and ultimately outlast them.

Now, understand that being comfortable with fluctuations is NOT the same as being comfortable with losing money. I want to be clear about that so you don't get the wrong idea.

When your market fluctuates, you don't actually lose money. Your property may no longer be worth as much. Yet that drop in value is only a true loss if you sell. If you avoid selling and patiently hold your property, the loss will only exist on paper. This means you haven't actually lost anything. So there's no reason to be uncomfortable.

In fact, despite the fluctuations, you may even be ahead.

You'd be ahead, despite the supposed loss, if you had a tenant. This is because the tenant would be paying you rent, thereby helping you to pay down the mortgage. With the mortgage being paid, you'd be on your way to owning the property outright. Your progress toward ownership would be a real, tangible gain. Thus, you'd be getting ahead, achieving an actual gain compared to the unrealized paper loss.

In addition, once the market finished its correction, you'd likely see your property return to its original value and then exceed it. This reflects the forgiving nature of real estate. As I keep saying, it's all a matter of giving yourself enough runway. If you can give yourself enough runway, the real estate market will forgive you.

Forgiveness means that the market will allow you to recoup your losses and then get ahead, on even the worst investments.

As an example, suppose I hideously overpaid for a property in Vancouver. I'd be making a bad investment, right?

Only if we looked at it in today's terms.

Looking to future, however, we'd recognize that an overpriced property today always seems like a bargain later, with enough time. This isn't just a quirk in Vancouver's real estate market either. No, just look at other major cities.

New York is case in point. Anyone who bought and held "overpriced" properties in NYC during the 70's and 80's is now laughing all the way to the bank. That's because yesterday's "overpriced" properties are now worth infinitely more. The value of these Big Apple properties has increased by so much that the old prices seem unreal.

If the New York example seems a bit exceptional, here's a more down-to-earth one. The example reiterates some earlier material while illustrating again, real estate's forgiving nature.

As an example, imagine you buy a house today for $250,000. Within two years, however, the house is worth $225,000.

Time to sell?

Nope. Instead, it's time to be patient. For as we've said before, your loss is not realized unless you sell. And at this point, there's no need to sell the property. If the property is rented out and you're collecting monthly income, your property's market price becomes meaningless. Ignoring the market price, your true focus is on the monthly income or cash flow your property produces. You're also thinking long-term, recognizing that your capital gains on the property, over time, will be tremendous.

When it's finally time for you to reap those gains, then you'll care about your property's market price. This will be the point where you finally sell your property. Until then, though, the fluctuating price of your property is just background noise. You can tune in to the noise, getting mentally distracted by it. Or, you can tune out the background noise, staying focused and on track.

The choice is yours, but you can probably guess what long-term investors do. As you might expect, long-term investors tune out the background noise. They focus on the realities of cash flow, not the false realities of paper losses.

Long-term investors also recognize the opportunity present in market fluctuations. This goes a step beyond what we said about being comfortable with fluctuations. When you're a true long-term investor, you'll begin to recognize the "silver lining" in any dark clouds that come over the market. The silver lining in these "dark clouds" (i.e. downturns) is that they're prime opportunities for buying more properties. To use another well-worn cliché here, it's like when life gives you lemons and you make lemonade.

Crack open a history book and you'll find this idea validated through-out history. Time and again, individuals have made vast fortunes by scooping up assets at a low price during massive downturns. From the Great Depression to the global financial "meltdown" of 2008; downturns have consistently offered a chance for savvy investors to get ahead. You can capitalize on similar downturns by acquiring assets and then patiently waiting for the market to return to normal.

Waiting patiently? There's that idea again, patience. It's absolutely critical to success in real estate. Yet so many aspiring investors can't be patient. We've just seen one way that these investors lack patience - being impatient with the fluctuations in the market.

Another way that impatience rears its ugly head is with respect to time. The investors who fail often lack the patience to spend time devel-oping assets. As a result, they never create a means of generating passive income, and ultimately reaching financial independence.

If only these aspiring investors would understand: there are no short-cuts to passive income. It takes time to develop.

You'll understand this once you get en route to building passive in-come for yourself. In your first eight to ten years, you won't notice much progress. You'll spend this time steadily acquiring and renting out prop-erties, following our steps from the previous chapter. It'll be slow going but hang in there.

Eight to ten years in, passive income will start to have a noticeable impact on your life. You'll start to see that you're paying off much of the monthly mortgage payments on your property/properties and chipping away at the principal. This will mean a greater positive cash flow for you, with less money going to interest.

And then, after about fifteen years, everything will begin to come together for you. This is where you reach the "promised land" of passive income. It's a point where you're not worrying as much about money and what the future holds.

By this time, if you've started young, you're in your late thirties or early forties. You're still working but have cash flow coming in from your investments. These investments have compounded over time, gradually forming a massive, income-generating "snowball".

Trust me when I say that having passive income really does make life easier and less stressful. I'm speaking from experience on this. About ten years ago, I began to see truly passive income. Each week and each month, dividend checks came in from my stock holdings and rent checks were coming in from my tenants. Both of which were building up my cash reserve. The feeling of receiving this income without doing any active work was exhilarating. So too was the sense that I didn't have to worry as much about where to get more cash. I knew that the cash would come to me, passively from my investments. Talk about having a feeling of security.

So why don't more people reach this moment - when passive income visibly kicks in and life becomes easier? It all comes back to a lack of patience. And in this case, being impatient means not accepting the time required to achieve passive income.

This second type of impatience seems initially rooted in our desire to always be doing something. Ever heard that cliché about "idle hands"? It's a testament to the society we live in, where being busy is seemingly a virtue.

With busyness held in high regard, we respect, for example, the executive who has a phone practically glued to their ear. Their busy life seemingly makes them important and successful.

While I can't speak to the situation of every person like this, I would question how much of their time is actually productive. We tend to confuse being busy with being productive. And the two are definitely not the same.

We still make that mistake, though, because we often find it intolerable to do nothing. That's not necessarily a problem when it pertains, for instance, to scheduling more events on an already-bloated social calendar.

It's a problem, though, in real estate. There, our constant impulse to fidget around does us no good. It may lead us, for example, to seek a "perfect" first property to buy, rather than one that's good enough to get in the market with. Or, if we're already in possession of a property, the temptation to always be active could lead us to sell the property too soon.

Fight this temptation whenever you feel it. Recognize that you don't always have to be doing more. In our first example, this means pulling the trigger and buying the property you've already found. And in our second example, fighting the temptation means sitting still for an extended period, so your property has time to appreciate.

The desire to always be busy is one reason I believe real estate investors frequently lack patience. Besides that, I'd also cite another cause: the so-called financial experts. I've blasted these guys in earlier chapters, but it never hurts to do so again. After all, they're bombarding you with their messages far more than I ever could.

Many so-called experts need to be taken to task because they contribute to the general impatience of the public on financial matters. You hear them do this, for example, on financial call-in shows. Tune in to many-a-show and you'll hear callers asking for opinions on stocks. The so-called experts then weigh in. Sell your shares of "X" stock, they advise. Or buy more shares of "Y".

How about "hang up the phone"? That's the advice I'd give the callers of these shows. Hang up because the "expert" on the show is giving advice without context. Mr. Expert usually knows nothing about the personal situation of the caller. Is the caller, for instance, just getting started with buying assets? Don't ask the "expert", they couldn't tell you. And this makes their opinions basically worthless.

Not only is the opinion worthless, but it also gives viewers the false sense that you can't patiently sit on your assets. Instead, you should monitor your assets, seemingly day and night, continuously questioning whether to sell them off.

That perspective keeps a steady stream of calls coming in to the "experts" on their shows. But it will keep a steady stream of income from coming in to your own bank account. Be patient, even as so-called experts promote impatience.

You must also be patient and tune out those "experts" who espouse "get rich quick" rhetoric. Again, I don't want to unload too much here. Too much of my own ranting and this book will change from a primer on financial independence into a diatribe against the "get rich quick" crowd. Let me just say though, once more, not to be enticed by the rhetoric on getting rich quick.

Following this rhetoric is like having a chocolate muffin for breakfast. Deep down, you know that both the muffin and the "get rich quick" rhetoric aren't going to give you anything of value. Both are empty, sugary things. Consume them and you'll experience a temporary surge of energy, before crashing later.

All this cutting on the so-called experts is to say that you need to ignore them. That goes for both sets of "experts". From those who give uninformed opinions, to the ones peddling "get rich quick" snake oil. Ignore either group and patiently work over time to become financially independent.

Moving on, let's cover a final mistake related to impatience in real estate. This type of impatience comes in relation to looking for quality properties. Time and again, aspiring investors aren't willing to spend time looking for quality assets to buy. Instead, they feel compelled to rush toward the low prices.

I'm all for a good deal, but quality is important too. In my opinion, it's better to buy a wonderful home at a fair price than to buy a fair home at wonderful price.

Actually, that's only partially my opinion. I'm putting a slight twist on what Warren Buffet says about stocks. Buffet, the "Oracle of Omaha", advocates buying wonderful stocks at fair prices rather than fair stocks at wonderful prices. In both his case and mine, quality wins the day.

Thinking about real estate, you can see proof of quality's importance in our previous discussion on location. Remember the example of the condo located above a twenty-four hour McDonald's? Or what about the condo near the bus turnaround? In both cases, you could buy the properties for less than ones of comparable size elsewhere. Yet the location detracted from the overall quality of these two condos, making them poor long-term investments.

Those two examples were in Vancouver, but you could just as easily find comparable cases in your own market. If, or when, you do; have the patience to keep looking. Don't be afraid to put in the time and effort needed to find a quality property. Ultimately, you'll be rewarded for your patience with high capital gains, greater ease in renting the place out, and many more benefits.

Patience, patience, patience - that's the key. Be patient, avoiding the three forms of impatience we've seen here. Do that and you're far less likely to "stumble" as you invest in real estate.

Having patience is important, yet it can be hard at times. To help you stay the course, here's an insight I have from my twenty-five years of working in real estate. During that time, I've met plenty of people who've bought and sold properties. Some have been my clients. Others have been friends, friends of friends, or just temporary acquaintances.

No matter who they are, however, I have never met anyone who bought a property, patiently held it for ten years or more, and then had regrets. But I have met hundreds of people who lacked patience and now regret selling their property too soon. Avoid similar regrets in your life and have patience.

Patience is fine, but what about those real estate secrets? I promised you my best "secrets" at the end of the last chapter and so far, haven't delivered any.

Don't worry, I'm getting to them now. We needed to cover impatience since it's the number one mistake I see real estate investors making. Now that we've covered all the gory details, let's go into those real estate "secrets" I promised.

Without further ado, here's the first one - build a support team.

Building a team may sound strange since this book is about how you, individually, can get into real estate. Yes, you need to take personal initiative and get into real estate for yourself. No question. But that doesn't mean you have to "go it alone". Instead, you should work to build your own high-quality support team. This team will support you, as needed, in your efforts to build real estate assets. Each team member will be able to do that as a result of having valuable knowledge and skills in a specific area.

The first person to get on your team is a good realtor. As we've said before, a good realtor has a healthy combination of general experience and specific experience in the neighborhood where you want to buy.

Additionally, if you're looking to buy an investment property, you should find a realtor who has experience buying these sort of properties. Make sure the realtor owns some investment properties themselves too. Otherwise, the situation is akin to buying a car from a car salesman who doesn't have a driver's license.

When you do find the right realtor for your team, be sure it's someone you can trust. The best relationships are those when you can trust your realtor to give you honest feedback and steer you toward the best units. This way, the only thing you'll ultimately have to question is whether or not to buy a given property. You won't also be questioning your realtor's judgment and intentions.

Once you've got a realtor, the next person for your team will be a mortgage expert. This expert can be a banker, a mortgage broker, or some other professional who specializes in getting people financed for real estate transactions.

Take the time to find the right mortgage expert for your team. You don't want to be sloppy about this. Trust me. I've seen too many people lose out on good properties due to bad financing.

It's a tragedy and one that seems to always unfold the same way. A buyer will come in with a deal that's subject to getting financing. Then the day before subject removal, the buyer suddenly finds that they can't get their mortgage put through. It doesn't matter why. The only thing that matters is that the deal won't go through.

Can you imagine how much this hurts? To find a property and be ready to buy it. Only to have the financing yank you back, at the last minute, like a bungee cord.

Suffice to say then, that it's important to have the right person (or people) helping you with financing. Carefully seek out a broker or bank who will work with you and help you avoid any unpleasant surprises when you're about to close a deal.

You should also choose carefully so you won't be steered into a narrow range of what you can buy. With the right broker, you'll have greater flexibility and range in your financing options. This enables you to have more options in terms of what you can buy.

Another point I'll make here, about finding the right broker for your team, is that all mortgage brokers and reps are NOT created equal. Some are more knowledgeable and more qualified to assist you than others. Your goal should therefore be to find and establish quality relationships with decision-makers at your bank.

This is what I've done over the years at Canada's two largest banks, TD and RBC Royal Bank. Years of work have given me trustworthy advisers at both banks who support my real estate efforts.

I say that now not to brag, but rather to reinforce the importance of building relationships with key people in financial institutions. Relationships put you in a far different position than simply walking up to a teller and asking for help with a mortgage. If you have to take that approach, walking up to the teller, you're dealing with a mere order taker. That's not meant to demean tellers. I have complete respect for them and find most to be quite competent. But if I'm trying to get financing for buying a property, I want someone with far more power.

At a bank, that person is usually a senior mortgage representative. Senior reps have the power to sign off and get you approved. These reps are not merely putting in requests, as a teller or other lower-down official might. Sending the request off to a distant head office.

The senior rep has actual power, allowing them to approve you and keep your deal from collapsing. For this reason, I believe it's essential to cultivate a long-term relationship with senior mortgage reps or their equivalents at your local bank. I'm in just such a position with the reps I mentioned. It allows me to have far greater flexibility in what I can consider and ultimately buy.

Easy for you, you say, but what about for people who are just getting started in real estate? How does a newbie get their own set of trusted advisors at the big banks to help with financing?

There's really two ways to do that. The first is to seek out advisors yourself. Dig in and find out who's the main rep or consultant at your bank. This takes time, but it can lead you to strong relationships.

I certainly didn't start off with connections at the banks. My first mortgage, for example, was with a junior-level rep. Yet I slowly figured out who the senior people were and then sought to establish relationships.

Then again, that's just one way to do it.

A far easier way to build relationships with financiers is to just ask your realtor. If you pick an experienced realtor, they'll likely have contacts in senior positions at the banks. And if not at banks, your realtor can probably put you in touch with financing professionals elsewhere.

A realtor. A mortgage broker. And now, the third person for your team - a tradesman.

Or rather tradespeople.

"Tradespeople" is a broad label for all of the specialists who'll help you to physically maintain your properties. These include plumbers, drywall installers, and electricians. You should also have multiple handymen in your arsenal of tradespeople.

Personally, I'd argue that a reliable, jack-of-all-trades handyman is probably the most important tradesperson you can have. These individuals can fix toilets, put in new light fixtures, repair tiles, paint, and much more. Their ability to perform the tasks, makes such handymen invaluable. You're bound to have a need for their services in some capacity with the properties you acquire.

The only problem is that handymen come and go. It's therefore imperative to get as many of them in your rolodex as possible. To do that, I recommend looking on Craigslist. You can also ask around, seeking out referrals from other property managers, condo organizations, and anyone else who's likely to use a handyman frequently.

Once you do find a handyman, look for ways to audition them. Think of it as auditioning the handyman for a role on your team, or in your rolodex of people to call on for help. Your "audition" can simply be a small, no-pressure job. The kind of job where you get a feel for the handyman without risking much.

A final person I'd recommend for your support team, at least eventually, is an accountant. Don't try to balance the books yourself. Get a professional accountant to do it for you. As with a financial expert, your realtor can probably refer you to a qualified accountant too. Just ask.

That does it for building your team. On to another real estate "secret".

The second "secret" I want to give you is this - go the extra mile, when buying or selling.

On the buying side, you can go the extra mile by taking initiative to find great properties. Look for example, to see which areas are being gentrified. Which areas and neighbourhoods do you see that are "up and coming"? If you can get into one of these neighbourhoods early, you're going to get an extra kick in appreciation over time.

Think about the meatpacking district in NYC, for instance. Anyone who got in there, buying property before the area became "hip", has made a fortune. This comes back to that long-term investor's mindset I keep impressing upon you.

It's also indicative of the philosophy of hockey star Wayne Gretzky. Gretzky had a magical ability on the ice because he never skated to the where the puck was. Rather, he went to where he thought the puck was going. This required extra work on Gretzky's part. But he was willing to go the extra mile in order to achieve success on the ice.

Real estate is no different. Like Gretzky, you've also got to go the extra mile when buying properties. Look for new neighbourhoods on the rise or unique properties in established areas. You can get a great feel for these neighborhoods and properties by biking around. Biking is my modus operandi, as it allows me to get some exercise and some good street-level intel. Bike if it's your style too, or feel free just to walk around. But do get out and have a look, one way or another. You're bound to make a better buying decision as a result.

As for selling, you can - and should - also go the extra mile here. When selling your property, go the extra mile by doing everything you can to ethically increase the marketability and the price. Clean up your property, making all necessary repairs.

If necessary, stage the property too. Staging means making the property presentable and attractive for those who come to showings. Often, staging can mean a five-fold return on investment from what you spend on staging versus what you can then make in selling your property.

To determine other ways you can enhance your property, always consult a realtor who specializes in listings. This happens to be my own area of expertise. As my clients can attest, I know how to bring out the most value in a property. Often, for example, if it will make a house complete, I may advise clients to finish out a powder bathroom. This renovation may cost them three to four thousand dollars. But the three to four thousand dollars spent now will complete the house. And it can mean fifteen to twenty thousand dollars later, when the property sells.

I may also recommend additional ways a client can increase their selling price. These ways include replacing a few light fixtures, de-cluttering inside, and landscaping and power-washing to improve the property's curb appeal. On curb appeal, you won't believe what a difference this makes. I've seen numerous cases where people have rejected perfectly great properties because they drove by and saw it was disheveled on the outside.

With all of these recommendations, my goal is to help my clients sell their property for the highest possible price. It's their home, after all, and I believe sellers (my clients) are entitled to every dollar they can earn from it.

Not every realtor shares my view, of course. And there are also realtors who don't know what it takes, in the first place, to enhance a listing's quality. Nonetheless, you can bet that there's still at least one realtor in your area who does share my view. A realtor who knows what to look for too. This kind of realtor is a listings and marketing pro. I'd encourage you to seek them out, when you sell a property.

Even if you don't go with a listing and marketing pro, you should still do whatever you can to enhance your property's value. It's all worthwhile, believe me. Any money spent will come back two-fold in the price you're able to get later. Plus, if you do everything you can, you'll never wonder whether you could have gotten a better price. That sense of wonder, and regrets too, will be non-existent because you've gone the extra mile.

Another real estate "secret" is to become well-rounded. This is one of the most important things I've learned over the years. I could never have achieved success in real estate and financial independence without working to become well-rounded.

By "well-rounded", I mean having a complex arsenal of knowledge in various areas. A fitting analogy here would be a UFC fighter. A UFC mixed martial arts (MMA) fighter needs to have many disciplines in order to succeed in the cage. This leads fighters to learn techniques from such diverse fields as wrestling, jiu-jitsu, boxing, grappling, and karate. A given fighter is unlikely to be world-class in every single element of all the disciplines they study. Yet the fighter will have a general, across-the-board proficiency which makes them absolutely lethal.

If you're going to score "knockouts" of your own, in real estate, you need to build up a similarly diverse arsenal. This will also keep you from having to rely on multiple people for too many other things.

To get your arsenal, go learn about real estate. Study subjects like buying and renting out properties, cap rates, and market values. Then get into learning about non-real estate investment too. In this latter area, educate yourself on topics like stocks, how to read a financial statement, PE ratios, tax shelters, and government pensions. And, if you really want to get an edge, verse yourself in physical maintenance. This means learning the basics of fixing things up. Learn how to repair tiles, fix toilets, install drywall, and more. You're not training to be a tradesperson, but studying these things will make it easier for you to work with them.

From real estate to non-real estate investment to maintenance - study it all. And know that you don't need to become an expert in everything. Like the UFC fighters, all you need is a working knowledge of each area. You'll then discover all the synergies between topics and how to combine them for an effective market "takedown".

Remember too, that you don't need to learn everything overnight. Take your time. View self-education for what it is - a worthy destination that takes years to reach. And even when you do seemingly arrive, there's always more to learn. So just relax and enjoy the feeling of growing progressively more intelligent and capable.

As you educate yourself, you want to be mindful of another real estate "secret".

This fourth "secret" is to be selective about information you follow. You need to be selective since you're going to be exposed to a myriad of sources while educating yourself. Not every source will be equally qualified to assist you. And you must recognize that.

In terms of who to trust, I'd say to only target people who have transparency. Look for people who have a clear track record of success in the area where you're seeking knowledge. Since success can be subjective, let's keep it simple. Only take advice from people who are multimillionaires and have done for themselves what they now advise others on. Seek out these people and steer clear of the anonymous "experts" lurking on forums. Anyone can give theoretical advice. But theory doesn't cut it if you want to become a successful investor. You want someone who's put the theories in practice and has success to show for it in the real world.

Another "secret", number five, is to pay yourself first.

Paying yourself first is essential so you have money to get in real estate. Without money, everything we've talked about in this book, especially in the last two chapters, will just be ideas swirling around in your head. The only way to make those ideas something more is to get money to invest and buy your first property. And that all starts by paying yourself first.

When you pay yourself first, you give yourself money before giving it to others. This means, for example, that money goes into your savings account before you spend it on a pair of jeans. You can still buy the jeans, of course. Provided there's money left over, after you've paid yourself. The same holds for spending money on restaurants, entertainment, and other non-essentials. Any of these non-essentials can be enjoyed after you've paid yourself, putting aside that first chunk of money in savings.

In terms of how much to put aside, I recommend saving fifteen to twenty percent of all the money you earn. This means you'd be saving approximately $15 of every $100 earned. Paying yourself first like this is essential to having the capital for investing. And the earlier you can start, the easier it is to do so, in the long run.

In my case, I started saving money at the age of thirteen. At the time, I didn't call it "paying yourself first". All I knew was that I couldn't spend all the money I made. Some of it had to go away and become untouchable.

If you're reading this now and panicking about how you haven't been saving, relax. It's not too late at all. There are plenty of self-made millionaires who didn't start saving meticulously at the age of thirteen. They save meticulously now, but it took a catalyst in adult life to get them in the habit of doing so.

I'm writing this book in the hopes that it can be your catalyst, on saving and other behaviors that lead to financial independence. Of those behaviors, another is to make decisions quickly, yet change your mind slowly. This behavior is so important that I'd label it as one of my "secrets" to success in real estate.

The first part of that, being able to make decisions quickly, comes from educating yourself and "doing your homework". If you develop yourself like that UFC fighter we mentioned, you'll be mentally quick when it comes to making decisions. Combine that with "doing your homework" on properties or a real estate market, and it's easy to decide with lightning speed.

Personally, I'm able to make rapid decisions when buying investment properties. As soon as I see the right unit come on the market, I can pull the trigger. This is because I know what I'm buying and the impact it'll have on my portfolio. I can make rapid decisions without regret because I know what I'm buying.

As for the second part of this, changing your mind slowly, that's a result of the long-term investor's mindset. A long-term investor is patient and avoids changing their belief system on a whim. That makes for an excellent "yang" to balance the "yin" of fast decision making.

The seventh "secret" I'll share with you is that money can buy happiness.

Uh-oh! I shouldn't have said that. Now you're going to think I'm Gordon Gecko (from the movie Wall Street), ready to tell you as well that "greed is good".

No, greed isn't good.

But money can buy happiness.

By "happiness", I'm not talking about being materialistic. What I'm getting at instead is the happiness that comes from having money work for you. People who have their money working for them are being carried along with little personal effort. This is the passive income we talked about earlier. It buys you time, so you can cut back on the amount of hours you spend working for money. It's why I titled my book "Along for the ride". And if you don't have to work as much for money - or even at all - do you think that will make you happy?

I'd hazard a guess that it would. Assuming that's true, your money buys you free time which leads you to be happy. So money therefore buys you happiness.

In order to reach that position, though, you've got to keep everything in focus, understanding how it all fits together.

In brief, what you're doing can be summed up in four overall parts. First, you're buying quality assets in real estate. A condo in an up-and-coming area would be an example of a quality asset. As you buy the asset, you're paying an attractive price relative to a conservatively estimated intrinsic value. This value is one you'll get a feel for from knowing a neighbourhood and from working with the right realtor.

Next, with the asset you buy, you're structuring it in a cost-efficient or tax-friendly way. Your realtor and accountant can advise you on how best to go about doing this.

They'll also help you with the third step, which is to arrange your overall portfolio so risks are intelligent and tolerable. On this point, my own recommendation is to structure the risk with twenty percent down, leveraging the other eighty percent. Structure your risk in this way and then rent your property/properties out. This way, what you get in rent will then cover your expenses and provide you with a bit of a buffer.

Finally, the fourth part of this overall process is to sit on your backside, avoiding the temptation to act. Don't think you have to be constantly fiddling with your investments. Sit tight and be patient.

If you've made it this far in the book, you certainly have the patience necessary to succeed in real estate. I say that because most impatient, wannabe investors would have stopped reading many chapters ago. The fact that you're willing to continue, even with all of the concepts I'm giving, indicates commendable patience.

It also indicates that you've got what it takes to attain financial independence. That's our ultimate objective in covering all of the topics in this book. With material like the "secrets" in this chapter, we're putting together a roadmap for financial success. The kind of roadmap that will help you become financially independent and free.

Real estate is a major part of our roadmap. Yet it's not the only part. In the next section, we're going to see a way outside of real estate in which you can build passive income. Any idea on what this method is? Take a guess and then join me for the answer, in Chapter 6.

Six

Dividends will slowly make you rich

"My formula for success rise early, work late, strike oil."

- J. Paul Getty, Oil Tycoon

"If you want any hope of retiring comfortably or even early then you have to get your money working for you. There are simply not enough working hours in the day to do it yourself."

- Owen Bigland

■　■　■

"This book is NOT about real estate."
Sound familiar?

It was the second sentence of this book. All the way back in Chapter One.

Think back to that first chapter. At the time, I promised you that this book wouldn't be exclusively about real estate. Yet if you've read up to this point, you've gotten a Thanksgiving-sized feast of all things real estate. Chapter after chapter of "meaty" content to help you get aboard the passive income "gravy train."

All of which seems to contradict that original anti-real estate slant. Are you confused?

Then check out this passage, also from Chapter One -

"And real estate? Well, that's part of how you become financially independent. Part of how you do it. Not the complete formula. Just one component."

See, there's a method to the madness after all. We've covered real estate, yes. But it's part of a larger discussion on how to create your own financial independence. A discussion which we're about to take in an exciting new direction. This chapter is going to depart from real estate entirely. We'll be entering uncharted territory, with a look at non-real estate investing.

To begin our discussion, let's define "non-real estate investments". This is a broad term, applicable to many different types of investments. You can use it to describe investments in everything from commodities (gold, silver, etc.) to tech start-ups to business franchises (McDonalds, GNC Nutrition, etc.).

You could also use the term "non-real estate investments" to describe physical items. Common examples would include art, antique cars, coin collections, or rare stamps.

Your "non-real estate investments" could even be antique guitars. Don't laugh. I have a friend who invests like this. Antique guitars are an integral part of his investment portfolio. My friend is so involved that he probably watches the guitar investor's equivalent of CNBC. He probably loses sleep too, whenever the antique guitar pundits - like those in real estate - give a "doom and gloom" forecast.

Personally, I've never had much interest in antique guitars or the swath of other non-real estate investment types. The reason is that, in most cases, you can't collect passive income from these investments. Look at my friend with the antique guitars. He doesn't receive any recurring income from these instruments. My friend may get immense satisfaction by owning a guitar that belonged to "The Rolling Stones". Yet that feeling won't pay his bills. Heck, the satisfaction alone won't even buy an item off McDonald's dollar menu.

I'm not necessarily disparaging on antique guitars as an investment. To each their own, really. I just prefer investments which pay while you hold them. Not investments that only pay when you finally sell them off.

For this reason, I've chosen to only invest in two specific areas. The first area is one that needs no introduction, real estate. By this point, you're hopefully aware that real estate pays while you hold it. This leads to the dream scenario we've discussed called passive income.

What you might not be aware of, though, is the second area where I focus on investing. That area is stocks. Like real estate, stocks are also a phenomenal way to create passive income and advance toward financial independence.

The magic of stocks is that they give you a "two-for-one" deal. Buy one stock and you get two ways of making money.

On one hand, you can make the money through appreciation over time ("capital gains"). This is when the value of your stock increases and you profit by eventually selling the stock.

Before you sell your stock, though, you have a second way of earning money. This is part two of our "two-fer" deal. Your second opportunity is with quarterly dividend payments.

A dividend payment will come to you whenever you buy stock in a company that pays its shareholders dividends. It's the company's way of thanking you for investing in them. Or more accurately, it's their duty, since buying stock makes you one of the shareholders they've agreed to pay. It's your share of the distributed profits.

Understand, though, that not all stocks are like this. Some stocks, especially those of growth companies in the tech industry, don't pay dividends. Therefore you must be mindful of the distinction between stocks that do and don't pay dividends. Otherwise you may watch your mailbox in vain for a check that's not coming.

But that's only if the stock you hold doesn't pay dividends. If it does, however, keep your eyes on the mailbox four times a year. At those times, you'll get a check for your share of the company's distributed net profits, paid as a quarterly dividend payment.

These payments will arrive in your mailbox with a consistency you can practically set your watch to. Coming to your mailbox or more commonly being deposited electronically into your brokerage account. They'll continue arriving, too, right on schedule, regardless of whether the stock market takes a nose dive. So long as the company itself is sound, its leadership will continue to pay you a quarterly dividend.

Oh, and here's the best part - you don't have to do anything. Your dividend payments are 100% passive income. It's comparable to how a tenant, in real estate, would give you a check for the rent each month. Unlike real estate, though, no additional work is required to receive a dividend payment. You don't have to screen tenants, fix leaky faucets, and occasionally stop by to say hello. The inanimate, formless stock couldn't care less about those things. All that matters to the stock and its company is that you own shares. Provided you do, you'll be paid a dividend. The dividend is a share of the profits the company has made for that quarter. And you're entitled to it as a shareholder/owner of the company.

If stocks pay you for no effort, why on Earth would anyone buy and rent out property? Seems silly, doesn't it, to go through all the effort of real estate investing. All that extra effort when you can buy a stock once and be done.

I can't argue with you here. If we're looking at real estate investing, in the rental sense, there's usually more work required. No question. Yet that work comes in exchange for leverage opportunities.

Leverage, does that ring a bell? If not, I'd recommend re-reading Chapters One and Three. Those chapters thoroughly cover leverage in real estate.

At the risk of being a broken record, all I'll say here is that leverage allows your money to go much further. You can get into real estate investments by paying just a fraction of their total cost.

Considering the power of leverage, it would be a mistake for you to avoid real estate and focus solely on stocks. Stocks are worthwhile as a form of investment with a low barrier to entry and little-to-no work required. The downside, though, is that you can only own what you can immediately afford to buy. A person buying stocks can't stretch their money, acquiring complete assets for less than the total cost. A real estate buyer, in contrast, does have this power.

Not that you have to choose.

I certainly haven't. As I mentioned before, my investments are in both real estate and stocks. Both of these asset types provide me with healthy levels of passive income. I receive this income in the form of rent checks and dividend payments.

Plus, each of my assets is steadily appreciating (increasing) in value. That means I could sell off shares of stock and properties for more income. I don't recommend it, though. Too short-term a play, at least in my opinion.

Ok, so real estate and stocks are both good. But which should you invest in first?

That's a personal decision. You'll probably be drawn to the stock market, though, at least initially. The stock market is much easier to get into.

I know this, from personal experience. My first investment was $1,000 of Pepsi stock. I made this investment over twenty-five years ago. At that time, I didn't have the down payment for a real estate asset like a condo. Actually, thinking back, I probably didn't even have the down payment for a closet within the condo. What I did have, though, was enough to get started with stocks. Buying Pepsi (the stock), I could therefore begin investing.

As I got my start with stocks, I'll admit that it did feel a bit scary. I was excited by the prospect of investing and earning passive income. Yet I couldn't ignore the fact that many investors seemed to be much smarter than myself.

I don't suffer from low self-esteem. But I've also never been a math prodigy. Nor would anyone accuse me of being the most technically-minded person. That's for the folks at places like M.I.T. and NASA.

What I do have is patience and the ability to think long-term. Thankfully, those abilities are what really counts in investing.

Having Einstein-like math skills doesn't hurt, of course. Yet you don't have to be good with numbers to be a successful investor. Your success has far more to do with your own ability to plot a long-term course and then patiently stick with it. That goes for both stocks and real estate investing. Neither is as complex as you might expect.

If anything, the true difficulty lies in staying the course. Especially when investing in stocks.

The situation in stocks brings to mind two lines from "If", a poem by 19th century author Rudyard Kipling. Kipling wrote The Jungle Book and probably never bought stocks. But he sounds like a seasoned investor saying, "keep your head, when all about you are losing theirs" and "trust yourself, when all men doubt you."

Kipling's words perfectly convey what it means to stay the course with stocks. "All about you" are going to continually lose their heads over the fluctuations in the stock market. It's therefore important to "keep your head", holding your stocks amid the chaos. As you do, those who are panicking may doubt you. But you must continue to trust yourself.

If you can keep your head and trust yourself in life, "you'll be a man" (according to Kipling's poem). And, if you can do it in the context of stocks, you'll be a mature, successful investor.

Keeping your head and trusting yourself with stocks means "out-thinking" other people. Not in the sense of having Warren Buffet-like genius. Rather "out-thinking" others by having a vision that dwarfs theirs. Most people envision stocks as something to hold temporarily. A few months, up to perhaps a year or two. You, on the other hand, need to see stocks on a vast multi-decade continuum. View stocks with thoughts of the next 30, 40, or 50 years.

When you do, you'll be able to see beyond the chaos of a single "flash in the pan" news event. Average stockholders can't escape this chaos. They fixate on it because their minds cannot conceive of a larger time frame.

Thinking in weeks, and months; these stockholders feel the news event is game-changing. It seems like a vast tsunami, rising suddenly and leaving lasting devastation.

If they could only think longer-term - a few years out - then the apparent tsunami would begin to shrink. Eventually, if these stockholders thought on the scope I'm advising you to, they wouldn't see a tsunami at all. The terrifying wave would only seem like an unwanted brush of the tide. The kind that gently nudges your feet, wetting them as you stroll along a beach.

Now, realize what I'm saying here. I'm NOT trying to downplay the tragic headlines you see each day. Terrorist attacks, virus outbreaks, bloody government coups - all of it is a big deal when it happens. Each time I read about such events, my heart goes out to those who've suffered.

Yet that's my heart. And I don't make investment decisions with my heart. I make them with my head. Thinking with a long-term investor's mindset and seeing stocks - as you must - on a timeline that spans for decades. A timeline where tragic headlines, along with less-tragic ones like Vancouver's new foreign buyer's tax - barely register.

As an investor, these events should only register to you as good buying opportunities. When they occur, it's like the stock market is having a sale.

"For one day only, save 30% on all companies in our health section!"

You can practically hear that pitch, for example, whenever there's a mass recall of a prescription drug. It's the kind of "sale" you don't want to miss. And you won't miss similar "sales" if you can just think long-term. Seeing that multi-decade continuum, and "out-thinking" most people in the process.

Another important piece of advice on stocks, and other non-real estate investments, is to "buy low and sell high". This means that you buy an asset like a stock, when it's valued as "low" within the price range you've set. Then, when you want to sell the asset, you first check that it has a "high" value - again, within your own range. If the asset's value isn't what you deem to be "high", you put off selling. Rather than sell, you continue to hold the asset, waiting patiently until you deem its value to be "high".

If this all sounds subjective, that's because it is. "Low" and "high" are each subjective terms you'll define for yourself. Don't worry about that subjectivity, though. Regardless of your definitions, there will always be assets for you to consider as long-term buys. And, for those assets which aren't in your range, you just need to be patient. Markets correct, assets depreciate, and you'll eventually see an opportunity to buy these out-of-range assets.

When you do buy an asset, I recommend holding it indefinitely. This is my policy, for example, with the stocks I hold. I rarely ever sell a stock. Instead, I prefer to hold the stocks and let them keep paying quarterly dividends.

An analogy for this would be a chicken, covered in barbecue sauce, roasting on a spit. As it roasts, mouth-watering drops of the barbecue sauce fall from the chicken. Scraps of meat occasionally fall off too. Neither of these by-products makes for a full meal. Yet they provide a reliable, effortless way to enjoy the chicken. A way that saves you from literally getting your hands dirty.

Eventually, you might choose to eat the chicken. If you did, it would be comparable to selling off stock. At that time, you'd stop receiving the savory by-products from the chicken - much as the sale of a stock would end your dividend checks.

I don't know about you, but I like getting dividend checks in the mail or in my brokerage account each quarter. It's income I haven't had to actively work for. If you do need the cash, sell off your stocks (or other assets). Hopefully you don't have to do that, though, as it comes with a huge tax bill and represents a huge step backward.

A better course is to hold on and let your assets keep running. Even better, redeploy your dividends from the assets, into more stocks and equities. That's how you build a "snowball". There's always opportunities to redeploy your dividends and make your money work for you.

Eventually you'll hold enough dividend paying stocks that you can simply live off the income. This would be the case, for example, if you had a portfolio worth two million dollars and the combined average dividend yield was 4%. The portfolio would therefore be paying $80,000 in dividends each year. The $80K in dividends would be your income from the portfolio. It would be indexed to inflation, about two or three fold, since the dividend growth rate runs at six to eight percent each year. So as a result, your principal (the $2M) would remain intact and you'd never EVER run out of money.

Sounds great, doesn't it? But it can be hard to keep this vision in mind amid the noise of The Street.

That's Wall Street, a place infested with traders. I say "infested" because the short-term mindset of traders bugs me. It'll bug you too. All you have to do is spend some time in the market.

When you do, you'll hear traders frantically scream to sell a stock, right when it's beginning to take off. Then, after they've sold, you'll hear traders justifying their short-sighted move. They'll claim that no one ever gets hurt by taking a profit. Or repeating for the umpteenth time that it's best to quit while you're ahead.

"Quit while you're ahead"? Sounds like something you'd hear at the blackjack table in Vegas. If you were hanging out with gamblers. And gamblers are essentially what most traders are. They treat the stock market like a casino, a place where success seems like a lucky dice roll. If you do get lucky, you've got to cash out ASAP. Otherwise, you stand to lose everything. The house always wins, remember?

In the casino, maybe. But not when it comes to investing. With investing, it's best to stay in the market for as long as you can. Continue collecting dividend payments or other passive income from the assets you hold. As you do, you'll be building wealth and the framework for your own financial independence.

While we're at it, talking about non-real estate assets, I want to clarify a phrase you've probably heard.

"Diversify your portfolio."

It simply means that you shouldn't "put all your eggs in one basket". Rather than a single basket, you should put your "eggs" in numerous "baskets".

One form of diversification would be through geography. You could diversify geographically, acquiring assets in both North America (U.S., Canada) and other regions. You might also diversify across industries or market sectors. Diversification in this sense would mean buying assets in multiple fields like commodities, pharmaceuticals, or biotech.

As an investor, I believe you should have some exposure to most - if not all - of the various sectors and geographic markets. Having across-the-board exposure like this, gives you a truly diversified portfolio.

Personally, I practice what I'm preaching here by using index investing. This means I'm buying a broad index or basket of stocks. My broad purchase forms a foundation for my portfolio. Then, I'll layer individual stocks from various sectors on top of it, spicing up the portfolio as I go.

In building my portfolio, I'm always careful to keep a cash emergency fund. This is something that you must also do as an investor. Maintain your emergency fund for those times when it's not just a rainy day, but an all-out hurricane. In those moments, you can draw on your emergency fund and continue to hold your investments. You won't be forced to sell investments for quick cash, at whatever the current market conditions are.

Emergency funds are essential, yet there's nothing glamorous about them. In fact, this whole notion of slow, careful investing probably seems downright boring. It probably doesn't fit with the image you have of successful traders. Those wolves of Wall Street. The ones you see earning six figures or more. Leading a lifestyle of the rich and famous.

I won't comment on the lifestyle. To each their own. What I can say is that there's often more to the successful traders than what you see. I don't mean drugs, back-stabbing, or the kind of shockers you'd find in a tell-all book. My point is that if you really look at it, these traders are playing a losing game.

The reality of active traders is that over eighty percent of them can't beat the index in any given year. Despite working fifty hours each week, these traders - again over eighty percent - still fall short of the return on indexes like the S&P 500. Of the twenty percent who do beat the index, it's usually by a very narrow margin. A margin which gets even smaller once you've deducted trading costs. Meaning only a handful of traders are honestly beating the market in a particular year.

This minority of a minority, if living the lavish "trader's life", should order plenty of bottles next time they visit a nightclub. They'll need the alcohol to dampen the pain of not being able to beat the market again. For the chances of lightning striking twice (i.e. beating the market), get even slimmer with each passing year.

So yes, the traders you see - those Jordan Belforts and Gordon Geckos - are rich. Yet they're playing a losing game in the long run. And these guys are also "rich", as opposed to financially independent. Rich, meaning there's plenty of money today but no certainty of it being around tomorrow. Especially with the way many of these traders burn through cash.

Let them be rich. For today. We're working towards wealth, for tomorrow and beyond. Financial independence too, so we can live comfortably without putting in a trader's fifty hour work week.

Non-real estate assets are part of how you achieve this wealthy, financially independent life. In this chapter, I've given you a basic overview of such assets. Continuing on, we'll be diving into the specifics of buying stocks. You'll learn the exact strategies I've used to build a passive income-producing portfolio. Best of all, you'll see how easy it is to take my strategies and apply them yourself.

See you on the next page, in Chapter 7.

Seven

How the stock market really works and building your portfolio the right way

"It's far better to buy a wonderful company at a fair price than a fair company at a wonderful price."

- WARREN BUFFET, FAMED INVESTOR AND WORLD'S
SECOND RICHEST MAN

"Ask yourself: Am I an investor, or am I a speculator? An investor is a person who owns business and holds it forever and enjoys the returns that U.S. businesses, and to some extent global businesses, have earned since the beginning of time. Speculation is betting on price. Speculation has no place in the portfolio or the kit of the typical investor."

- JOHN C. BOGLE, VANGUARD FOUNDER

■ ■ ■

Will you be shocked?
Angry?
Depressed?
I can't say.
But I'll bet you never look at stocks the same way.
Not after reading this chapter.
It'll be the adult equivalent of finding out that Santa Claus isn't real. (Seriously, he's not!)
No need to over-hype this, though. You get the point.
Now let's get your blood boiling.
I want to let you in on a closely-guarded secret of the financial industry. This is a secret that most financial professionals absolutely do not want you to know.
It's the secret of how successful and wealthy people actually invest their money.
If you look at such individuals, you notice that they invest in two basic ways. First, they buy and hold quality real estate for long periods of time. We've covered that in our own discussion across earlier chapters. So it's probably not a huge shock to you.
The shock, though, lies with the second way that successful and wealthy individuals invest. They buy shares in quality companies and then hold the stock for extended periods.
And?
And that's it.
In most cases at least.
The individuals we're describing don't - at least on a basic level - do much else with stocks. They're certainly not glued to Bloomberg, distracted by the parade of four-letter symbols across the stock ticker. Nor are they yelling four-letter words every time the ticker shows that a stock they own is down.
What makes this reality shocking is that it's the complete opposite of what most financial professionals advise. Ask one of these "professionals" for advice on stocks and they'll encourage you to be continually trading. You should be buying companies, holding the stock for a few weeks, making some money (hopefully), and then selling your shares to buy a

different company's stock. Over and over again. It's called the churn and it's what keeps stock brokers in business. They have to keep you trading. Otherwise, they don't see a commission.

Yet as we've said, wealthy and successful people are NOT constantly buying and selling stocks. It's not how they invest.

Maybe financial professionals - by the thousands, no less - are just unaware.

Yeah, maybe.

But I'd wager those in the financial industry are very, very aware. They're aware of what it takes to succeed with stocks. And they're also aware that knowledge of what it takes directly threatens the existing commission system. A system by which brokers, stock advisers, and other financial professionals get paid each time their clients do a trade.

Since they get paid when you trade, the financial industry has every reason to conceal the truth about success with stocks. They want would-be investors to believe that trading is the key. That way, the commissions for each trade keep flowing in.

Yet you don't need to be trading nearly as often as those in the industry would suggest. It's also not essential for you to have a financial professional, "help" as your stock adviser.

I say "help" (in quotes) because the financial industry seems to have its own unique definition of the word. Somehow, they've arrived at this alternate definition despite what's in Webster's dictionary. If you're curious, the financial industry seems to define "help" as "to bamboozle and swindle, while keeping a straight face."

Oh, was that harsh? Unnecessary too.

Well so are the commissions you'd be paying for financial "help". These commissions can be harsh and they're definitely unnecessary.

The only reason people pay such fees is because they believe the stock market is an enigma. Any guesses who we have to thank for that impression?

Could it be the financial industry?

I'd say.

Stocks have to seem confusing. Otherwise, those in the financial industry won't be "wizards" to their clients. Instead, their clients won't be clients. They'll be off investing independently.

For those who know movies, the situation is like The Wizard of Oz. The financial industry (much of it) is an imposing "stocks wizard". Until that is, you look behind the curtain. Then, like Dorothy in the movie, you see a scrawny guy with some special effects.

Can't have that, can we?

Actually we can. And that's among my motivations in writing this chapter. I want to expose the deception and completely change how you look at stocks.

If you want to succeed with stocks, then forget about the day-to-day price of a company's stock. You won't be trading day-to-day, so this price is irrelevant. Your focus should be directed instead toward what stocks you actually own. Think about the income that these stocks can produce for you, annually.

As you do, you'll be in good company. It's the behavior of successful and wealthy investors.

Another of their behaviors is to avoid mutual funds. A mutual fund is an actively managed "basket of stocks". It's also a blatant ripoff. For the reason that, as noted in the last chapter, the vast majority of traders can't beat the market. So you're paying for an investment that will nearly always under-perform. Plus, adding insult to injury, mutual funds charge a management expense ratio (MER). This is a commission charged every year to run the fund. It can range from 1% to approximately 3.5%.

Those percentages don't sound like much, yet consider what they'll equal over many years. Suppose, for instance, that you put away $500 per month in a managed mutual fund with 2% MER. You'd begin in your 20's, so as to have a comfortable return by the time you retired. And, no doubt, you'd have definitely made some money by retirement age (65). Your managed mutual fund, at this point, would be worth $325,000.

Still, consider what your return would be if the same $500 per month were placed in an index ETF fund with a low fee. An example here would be the Vanguard S&P 500 ETF. It charges you between 6 and 30 basis points. That's a far cry from managed mutual funds, which typically charge 200 basis points.

On a side note - Vanguard's fund is called an ETF, or "exchange traded fund". It's an investment tied to an index such as the S&P 500 (in the U.S.) or the TSX 60 (in Canada). Being linked to an index means ETFs rise and fall based on the overall pattern of one particular index.

For most beginner investors, that's just fine. Most people will do well with just index investing. Buying ETFs from Vanguard or iShares (Blackrock).

How well can you do with an ETF? Let's return to our example, with Vanguard. Using Vanguard's ETF, your return at age 65 would be $600,000. You'd have made nearly double the return of the mutual fund.

Can you see now why master investors don't touch mutual funds? They recognize how much of your profit, the managers of these funds end up taking over time. Plus, once again, the managers get paid regardless of whether the stocks in the fund even do well.

As an analogy, it would be like paying someone to remodel your home, regardless of how the home looked afterward. The remodeller could devastate your house, turning it into a filthy, toxic dump. They could also overcharge you for the work and then add ridiculous fees like $100 for nails. And you'd happily pay them everything they asked for.

Crazy right? You'd never let a remodeller get away with this. So why allow a fund manager, someone who's "remodelling" your portfolio, do the same?

That's not meant to be rhetorical, by the way. The answer is that you shouldn't. Even if by some chance, you still want to work with a mutual fund manager, at least be aware of their atrocious fees. These fees are an investor's worst enemies. You'll face fees when working with a mutual fund manager and also with a traditional stockbroker too.

In the stockbroker's case, you'll be charged fees whenever you want to buy and sell a stock. Expect to pay at least $100 to $150 for such trades. This tends to be the average, though I've seen exceptions where brokers give "discounts" of $60 to $70 per trade.

Avoid those trading fees with an online discount brokerage. The one I use, TD Waterhouse (a.k.a. TD Ameritrade in the U.S.), charges just $9.99 per trade. The catch is that I'm doing my own trades electronically, online. But it's hardly a complicated task. Especially if you approach it with the kind of independent spirit advocated throughout this book. Educating yourself on how to do trades and then taking action.

TD Ameritrade isn't the only online discount brokerage either. There are scores of others, with Schwab's being another good pick.

While I'm making recommendations, let me touch on investment strategy too. I recommend an overall strategy of index investing, with a layer of dividend growth investing over top. This is my own strategy and I highly encourage you to follow it.

I'll be showing you more about the strategy later in this chapter. Before then, here's something else you should know - index investing and dividend growth investing takes time. You'll need to spend at least some time with set up and monitoring.

If you don't have the time, I'd recommend you hire a fee-based adviser.

Hire someone? After I've just insulted the financial industry?

Yes, and here's why it's not a contradiction. Your fee-based adviser isn't paid by commission. The number of trades you do isn't going to take them from a Honda Civic to a Ferrari. Rather, as the name suggests, a fee-based adviser works at a flat fee. It's similar to hiring a lawyer or an accountant. You pay the adviser a fixed, hourly rate to set up your portfolio. The adviser's work saves you time in the present. It also saves you hundreds of thousands of dollars, over your investing lifetime. Your savings come from not paying broker's fees and commissions, often for performance that lags the index.

In case it's not clear to you by now, I'm not a fan of many so-called "investment professionals". My disdain comes, in part, from what we've discussed so far on fees that don't match actual performance. I'm also turned off by the way these "professionals" misrepresent their abilities in advertisements.

I'll see their ads at home in Vancouver. The ads often claim an advisor makes smart investments. The kind that lead to superior returns, despite these "turbulent" times.

On the surface, this sounds plausible. Maybe the advisor does have some sort of Midas touch. But if they do, why does the advisor need to run ads? Shouldn't they be well-known as a genius at beating the market?

These "geniuses" shouldn't have to pay for ads telling people about their abilities. It should be common knowledge. The advisors should also have clients galore and be on the cover of major magazines. You'd see them on the covers of Barrons, Fortune, and Forbes. Frankly, you'd expect them to be long retired too, living off the millions they made.

Yet where are they? The apparent "geniuses". These so-called "investment professionals". Instead you see them paying for ads on the radio and in the newspaper. Ads to get the word out and attract clients. Ads offering a free consultation, no less.

A free consultation?

Would Warren Buffet - arguably the greatest investor of all time - give free consultations to anyone who called his office?

He might have done it, decades ago as an upstart. When he had no track record. Before he had become a legend, the so-called "Oracle of Omaha". But now, it would be laughable for Buffet to put ads in a local paper and offer free consultations.

Speaking of Buffet, he's also not a fan of fake investment pro's. The kind who falsely claim they can outsmart the market. In fact, Buffet was so aggravated that he went on TV and issued a 10-year challenge. The "Oracle of Omaha" challenged any fund manager to beat the performance of his own simple investments over a 10-year period. If the manager could do so, Buffet would award a one million dollar prize.

Eventually, a challenger stepped forward and took him on. The challenge began, with Buffet simply buying the S&P 500 index. His challenger, in turn, engaged in a variety of complex investment maneuvers.

Fast forward to the present and the challenge is now entering its ninth year. Buffet's holdings for the bet are up 20% now, over those of his challenger. With just a year to go, that lead is virtually unbeatable. Buffet has essentially won.

Buffet's victory proves the power of simple investments. Simple investments can often produce far better returns than more complex ones made by the "investment professionals". And if that's the case, why pay someone ungodly sums to invest on your behalf? Why not just educate yourself a bit and then make some good simple investments?

One way to do that - which I alluded to earlier - is with index investing.

Index investing is where you buy an entire index, such as the S&P 500. If you bought the S&P, you'd own a share in all 500 of its companies. Not a bad investment since these companies are 500 of the largest in the U.S. Beyond that, the sheer variety of S&P companies gives you tremendous diversification. Your investment "eggs" are most assuredly not all in one basket.

Index investing does have a notable drawback, though. The drawback is that you can't separate between good companies and bad ones. Not when you buy the entire index. You're scooping up all of the companies together. And not all of them will perform as winners. But then could you really expect all 500 companies in the S&P, for example, to be champs every single year? Of course not. What you can expect is that index investing will give you a stable foundation for your portfolio. A foundation that neither you nor any fee-grubbing fund managers need to tinker with.

For most people, index investing is all they need - at least with respect to stocks. Just buy an index and hold it. You don't need to also churn through individual stocks. By churning, I mean constantly buying and selling the stocks in your portfolio. In effect, churning the portfolio around every few months. Financial "pros" are strong advocates of churning. Yet as I've said - and Warren Buffet has proven - those guys should often be ignored.

If you do wish to go beyond just buying indexes, avoid churn. In its place, I'd recommend you follow a strategy of dividend growth investing.

Dividend growth investing is when you buy a company that not only pays quarterly dividends, but also has a long, uninterrupted history of increasing them. The advantage for you the investor, is that you receive a dividend payment each quarter, and that payment increases every year.

As you receive your dividends, you then reinvest them in other dividend-paying companies. Over time, you acquire enough companies that their quarterly dividend checks (paid on different schedules) seem to come every week.

Imagine getting paid for no work every single week. Do you think it would be easier to stay the course and not get swept up in the short-term trader's mentality? You'd have no reason to descend into that madness because your investments would already be paying you. While others despaired, you'd be seeing tangible gains every single week.

As you think about dividend growth investing, it helps to know what an increasing dividend means. When a company increases its dividend, it indicates that the company is healthy and profitable. That's because the company's dividends are based on earnings and profit growth. So with an increasing dividend, the company is generating enough free cash flow to retain profits for R&D, acquisitions, and stock buybacks, while also paying out even more money to its shareholders.

The dividends a company pays you will come, right on schedule, like clockwork. This is why I liken dividends to a base salary. It's something you can depend on, even if the stock market stays flat.

FACT - On a pre-tax basis, dividends have accounted for 46% of the total return on the S&P 500 index over the past 25 years.

When the market performs well, you'll get capital gains - earning money from price increases in whatever stocks you hold. Those capital gains are like a bonus. A payment that comes, as in the working world, from good performance.

Much as you may like capital gains, though, you can't live on them. Nor can an employee - in most cases - live solely off their bonus. You need something more reliable to stay the course. Like dividends.

Another point of dividends, mentioned briefly in the last chapter, is that they pay consistently. Even when the outside market suffers. The market could take a 20-30% correction, for instance, and you'd still be collecting your dividend checks. It's comparable to real estate, where your tenant's monthly payments matter and the outside market's performance doesn't. Dividends and monthly rent each insulate you in their own respective ways against the chaos of the market.

I recommend dividend growth investing to you because it's what I've used myself for over twenty years. Thus far, I've been quite pleased with my returns. Follow my lead with dividend growth investing and I know you'll be just as happy.

To help you follow my lead, I'd now like to share the steps of how you get started. Not in general. No, the exact first steps you can take to get started as a dividend growth investor.

First things first, you simply open an online trading account with a bank. Setting up the account is almost always free. Many banks then usually start you off with five to ten free trades. Once you've made those trades, you're typically charged about $9.99 per additional trade.

With your trading account set up, it's time to think about buying stocks. I say "think about" because it's in keeping with our careful, deliberate investor's mindset. You should think before buying any stocks. Your thoughts, in turn, should come after doing market research. Only then will you be in a position to make a clear, educated decision.

To start your research, check out David Fish's Dividend Champions list. This list contains approximately 100 companies that have raised their dividends for a minimum of 25 consecutive years. Many of the companies have even raised dividends for 30 to 40 consecutive years.

You can also refer to a second list, the S&P 500 Dividend Aristocrats list. It features roughly 50 of the largest U.S. companies on the S&P 500. These companies have also raised dividends uninterrupted for over 25 years.

From the two lists, I've personally found a number of great companies to invest in. One of my favorites is Johnson & Johnson (J&J). Look at their performance and you'll see green. The reason is that Johnson & Johnson has averaged 5% to 8% growth in their dividend every year. Over time, with the dividend continuing to increase, you'll get a beautiful compound effect from owning J&J stock.

In looking at companies like Johnson & Johnson, you should be wary of reading too much into their day-to-day prices. These prices may vary wildly from one day to the next. Yet often, the changes in price have little to do with a company's own fundamentals.

Instead price swings may actually be the result of buying and selling in the market. In other words, a company itself would not be the reason why its stock price has gone up or down. The true culprit may be buyers and sellers, loading up or unloading company stock.

As evidence, consider that 90% of shares trading on the NYSE are from large institutional investors. Non-institutional investors - so called "Mom and Pops" - only account for about 10% of the market. This disparity means stocks are often vulnerable to the actions of a few individual institutional investors.

Imagine, for example, that a mutual fund manager decides to liquidate part of his portfolio. The manager, like many institutional investors, might hold ten to twenty-five million dollars or more of stock in a company. When he suddenly sells off all his shares, it's likely to have an impact on the stock's value.

The manager's actions could also cause other stockholders to sell their shares of the same company's stock. These stockholders might sell on the belief that the manager has an inside scoop on the company. Acting on this flawed hunch, the stockholders would then sell and further impact the company's stock price.

Don't make this mistake yourself. Recognize that most investors really don't have the inside scoop. They're unlikely to know something you don't. And if by some rarest of the rare chance an investor does have unique knowledge, don't worry. We live in an age of information overload - a time when new information freely flows to us 24/7. Meaning that today's "insider tip" may be common knowledge or even irrelevant tomorrow.

Besides, the lack of true "insider knowledge" is actually a good thing. It means you can relax. You don't have to break out in a cold sweat if a fund manager suddenly liquidates their holdings in a given company. You can rest easy, knowing the manager's behavior probably has nothing to do with the stock. Not with the stock's underlying value, anyway.

So why exactly is the fund manager selling? One reason might be that the manager has a large client wishing to get cash. In this case, the manager would liquidate their holdings in a company, so as to get the cash for redemptions and pay their client. Another reason could be that the manager themselves wants cash. Perhaps they see better buying opportunities elsewhere. By liquidating the stock, the manager can get the funds for their own subsequent investment.

These are just two examples, though. Of many, many, many more. Anything is possible really. The manager might even be crazy. It happens, after all, when you look at numbers bouncing around all day.

You don't want to go crazy too. So keep your eyes off the flickering prices and keep seller behavior in perspective. That way you'll ensure your own sanity.

In addition, you should also understand the true nature of valuations. On one hand, you should know that the valuations of a company's stock are not always correct. People like to think that the market is "efficient", but in the short-term it's often not. In the short-term, stocks may go for a time being overvalued or undervalued. This means that if you look at metrics like profit margins and dividend payout ratios; you can find some nice, undervalued stocks to purchase.

Having said that, most stock prices will ultimately correct, bringing their company to an accurate valuation. Over the long term, a company will reach or return to what it should be valued at.

You can think of this situation with valuations as the difference between a voting machine and a scale. I use this metaphor myself to help make sense of valuations. The way I see it, the stock market is a voting machine in the short-term. This is because, in the short-term, the public "votes" to determine what a company is valued at. Over the long-term, however, the valuation ceases to be based on votes. Instead, what matters are the core fundamentals of the company. These fundamentals determine which companies are the true heavyweights (no pun intended), able to outlast market fluctuations.

You're welcome to look for undervalued companies. It's one of the things that can make investing quite enjoyable. Just be mindful of not spreading yourself too thin. You don't want to suddenly own an unruly mess of 70+ stocks, many of which "seemed like a good idea at the time". I'd personally recommend you keep to 15 companies, 20 tops. That way you can have some gems in your portfolio without being overextended.

Which companies are gems? That's the ultimate question. One that everyone seems to have an answer for.

Personally, I'd start off describing a so-called gem as a company that pays a dividend. This dividend must increase every year too. Beyond that, I'd focus - at least initially - on five simple considerations.

These considerations form the crux of what I see as "quality" companies, worth investing in. As a service to you, I'd like to go into depth on them here - offering you a guide to selecting companies that are sound, profitable investments.

My first consideration is whether I can understand the company. Do they sell products or provide services that are clearly apparent? There is no mystery, for example, on Coca-Cola's business. They sell sugared water and other beverages to consumers around the world. Coke also has a healthy side business selling syrup or concentrate to other bottlers at a profit.

Makes sense, right?

Sure. But how about "Woo-Woo"? You know them right? They're the next big tech start-up. Featured in Inc. Magazine, Fortune, and a smattering of other top media outlets. Facebook and Google each want to buy "Woo-Woo" for billions. Venture capitalists and private investors all want a piece of the company too. But can anyone say how this profitless, eight month-old company makes any money?

No. Most likely not.

For those who haven't heard of "Woo-woo", don't worry. You're not living under a rock. There's no such company, to my knowledge. Instead, "Woo-Woo" is a ridiculous name that's meant to convey the equally ridiculous tendency of people to invest in unclear companies. The kind of companies which, recently, seem to come from the startup world.

Unlike Coca-Cola, there's often no clear profit engine in these companies. It's also frequently unclear what many such companies even do. For this reason, I call unclear companies "cult stocks". Anyone who invests in them seems to have drank a Kool-Aid that makes them incapable of thinking clearly. How else can you buy stock in a company you don't understand that's never been profitable? It's only possible with "cult stocks".

My advice is to avoid "cult stocks". Stick to companies like Coca-Cola, Hershey, or McCormick Spices. In all three of these cases, I probably don't need to tell you what each company does. Or how they make money. Even if McCormick doesn't ring a bell, you're probably tipped off by the "Spices" part of their name. These companies are all simple and profitable, with nothing cultish about them.

I've ranted a bit here, in talking about "cult stocks". But so do cult leaders, right?

Moving on, here's my next consideration when examining companies to potentially invest in. I'll look next to see whether the company has a wide competitive moat. Ideally, a company will be so big and so entrenched in a market that it's difficult for a competitor to come challenge them.

Think again about Coca-Cola. Could you see a competitor coming in today and creating a serious rival drink? A drink that would threaten Coca-Cola's $46 billion dollars in annual revenue (2014). Your odds of winning the lottery are probably better. Coke's competitive moat is just too wide for competitors to cross.

Would-be competitors will either run out of money along the way, figuratively "drowning in the moat". Or, Coke - and other companies in this position - will simply drop their margins, competing on price. This latter course is like lowering the drawbridge to crush and smother those in the moat. That might sound brutal, but entrenched companies like Coca-Cola are not about to give up their castle. Nor do they have to. Such companies have more than enough resources to thwart and outlast any siege. They are therefore likely to be strong investments.

Companies with wide competitive moats are also likely to be price makers. As an investor, you want price makers - those companies who largely determine what an item in the market will cost. An example is Apple with smart phones. In Apple's case, they develop the product (iPhones) and then charge a high price for it. Apple can justify this price on the grounds that their product is the best, therefore deserving premium pricing and superior profit margins.

Apple's stance differs from other companies who set their prices in reaction to the market. We call companies of this second type, price takers. Companies who are price takers must take whatever they can get, as pricing, from the market. They lack the ability to actively set their own pricing.

Examples of price takers are companies that sell commodities like oil (Chevron, ExxonMobil) or metals (BHP Billiton, Rio Tinto). In these cases, the company's fate is tied to its external commodity. No matter how well the company is managed, the commodity will ultimately determine pricing.

As an investor, you should generally avoid price takers, concentrating instead on price makers. The only reason to have a few price takers would be to add some diversity to your portfolio. I do this, for example, with ExxonMobil and Chevron stock.

Currently these two companies account for less than 5% of what's in my portfolio. That's definitely enough because most price takers don't consistently pay dividends every year. ExxonMobil and Chevron do pay consistent dividends but that's because they have retail operations too. Being in retail makes the two companies different from pure price takers like say, ConocoPhillips, and more resistant too.

Excluding these two exceptions, if you're after safe and increasing dividend payments and the passive income they provide, price takers usually can't help you. You should therefore keep them to a small percentage in your portfolio, concentrating instead on price makers.

As a rule, I would limit yourself to no more than 5% of price takers. Keep the percentage of price takers in your portfolio low because their dividends can be cut suddenly and without warning.

Also, on dividends, you should be mindful of the payout ratio. The lower this ratio is, the better. You don't want a company with an excessive payout ratio. Such a ratio would be anything over about 60%. Percentages exceeding 60% usually mean that a company is paying too much out in dividends and not reinvesting enough in its own growth.

There are exceptions, though, especially depending on the industry. The tobacco companies Altria and Phillip-Morris, for example, have payout ratios of approximately 70-80%. For them, these percentages are not unreasonable because the tobacco industry is limited today in the ways it can do marketing. This means that Altria and Phillip-Morris can't reinvest their profits to do more marketing, like companies in other industries can.

Speaking of reinvestment, it's typically a good sign whenever you see a company actively reinvesting its profits. Companies that actively reinvest are thinking about their future. Don't let them be the only ones. You should also think hard about what the future holds for any company you might invest in. This is my fourth consideration for a potential stock investment. I think about whether a company will still be profitable and relevant, two decades or more from now. Thinking about the future means, for example, that if it were the 1920's, I would invest with Henry Ford rather than a buggy company.

Think about the future, yet do so in moderation. You don't want to be so future-focused that you engage in speculation. What I'm suggesting here is simply to be mindful of where a company or its marketplace seems to be heading. This comes back to doing your homework on companies and being knowledgeable, in general, on the world around you.

A fifth and final consideration when examining companies is whether purchasing their stock will enable you to have more passive income flows. As an investor, this is why you're in the market to begin with. With each investment, you create another cash flow - essentially buying yourself a day or two of financial freedom.

One day of freedom could come from buying $3,000 of Johnson & Johnson stock. The company's dividend currently yields 3.5%, meaning you get paid $105 every year for as long as you hold it. Your $105 is equivalent, depending on your lifestyle, to the total amount of money required for one to two day's living expenses. As long as you receive this dividend, you don't have to work for money, for one to two days per year.

Plus, J&J is reliable. On average, they've had 6% to 7% dividend growth every year over the last 25 years. This means, for example, that your $105 earned this year will go to $112 or $113. The company may very well raise the dividend too, another few percents, above their average 6% or 7%. This is even better when you consider that inflation is only running at about 2.5%-3%. So with an average 6% to 7% dividend growth rate from J&J, you're covered by 2X against the rate of inflation. Now that's a good investment. One that will protect you. And, of course, one that brings you your financial freedom, one day at a time.

Speaking of financial freedom, a day or two of it is great, but why stop there? Keep going and see if you can make it to 365 days. A lifetime's worth of financial freedom.

Hit that target and you no longer need to work. Your investments will provide the passive income to cover your daily expenses.

If you want enough passive income for a year to cover all your annual living expenses, you should follow - or at least consider - the five criteria I've just given. Those criteria will make it easier for you to spot "quality companies" and add them to your portfolio.

In the interest of helping you even more, let's now dive even deeper into my personal investment approach. I want to show you the step-by-step process of how I select a stock. It's not nearly as complicated as you might expect either.

I usually begin by narrowing the field to stocks on the "Dividend All Stars" list. I may also consult a second, similar list of "Dividend

Aristocrats" - stocks on the S&P 500 that have not only paid a dividend, but also increased that dividend uninterrupted for 20 or more consecutive years.

Looking at these lists narrows down my search to perhaps 100 to 150 companies. Of these, I'll then begin looking for companies that meet a few specific metrics.

One metric is P/E (price-earnings). I want companies that have a P/E ratio of less than 20. If a particular company's P/E sits under 20, I'll then check their dividend yield. Hopefully, this stat is 2% or higher. If so, I'll focus in on the company's dividend payout ratio. I want the ratio to be less than 60%.

By now, my list of possible companies has shrank considerably. I'm certainly not dealing with 100 to 150 companies any more. No, it's more like a small handful.

From this handful, I'll make my final decision by looking at what sector each company is in and where I need exposure. My goal is to diversify my portfolio, balancing it against being over-invested and off-balance in any single area.

To do so, I need to be exposed, but not overexposed, to various areas of the market. I've done this in my portfolio by investing in companies across a variety of basic sectors.

In the spirit of transparency, let's take a brief look at each of my holdings by sector. As we do, keep in mind that I'm not recommending these specific stocks. What I hold may not necessarily be ideal for you. The takeaway for you lies in seeing how my portfolio fits together and then using it as guidance to build your own.

In my portfolio, consumer goods are the first sector in which I hold company stock. The specific companies here are: McCormick & Co, PepsiCo, Coca- Cola, Colgate-Palmolive, Procter & Gamble, Nestle, and Diageo.

Most of these companies are probably familiar to you, as they make the kind of day-to-day items our "survival" seems to depend on. I, for one, can't live without a little spice when cooking. And I'm sure you probably need your Coke or Pepsi, perhaps more than you'd care to admit. So buying stock in these sort of consumer goods companies just makes sense. They are well-established and very easy to understand. That's true even for Diageo, a company you may not recognize by name. Diageo owns Guinness, Johnnie Walker, Smirnoff, and a bevy of other alcohol brands.

Another sector in which I own stock from various companies is the financial sector. My holdings here are from: Royal Bank, Toronto Dominion Bank, Sun Life, and Wells Fargo. Each of these companies is large enough for my liking. Also, as they're in the banking sector, these companies all have a natural inclination toward stability and accountability.

You probably won't be surprised at the next sector in my portfolio. It's health care and includes a company you might be sick of hearing about - Johnson & Johnson. While you may be sick of them, Johnson & Johnson keeps me quite well. Both with Tylenol (when needed) and, of course, in terms of their dividend payments. Other stocks that keep me in good health from this sector are: CVS, Celgene, Gilead, and Eli Lilly.

My portfolio also includes stocks from some "unhealthy" companies too. That's "unhealthy" in terms of their products. Not in terms of performance. I'm talking about my holdings in the services/retail sector. Within this sector, one of my holdings is McDonalds. Now that's a quintessentially "unhealthy" company. But only if you look at Big Macs, McFlurries, and McNuggets. If you look instead at their stock, it may actually lead you away from a heart attack - rather than toward one. The same goes for my other services/retail sector companies - Costco, Walmart, Nike and Disney.

Looking at that last category (services/retail), you may see that I have a trend toward big, established, name-brand companies. That trend continues into my holdings for the industrials sector. For industrials, I hold stock from similarly prominent companies. These companies are: General Electric, Honeywell, 3M, Dow, and United Technologies.

My emphasis toward prominent companies also extends into the technology sector. Like Buffet, I'm not a huge tech investor. I can make an exception (or two) for Apple and Google. Companies like these can hardly be considered unstable, unproven upstarts.

I'd say the same for companies in the final two sectors of my portfolio - utilities/telecom and basic materials. The utilities/telecom sector companies I hold are Fortis, BCE, and Telus. As for basic materials, I'm invested here with stocks from Chevron and ExxonMobil.

Along with my holdings in those eight sectors, I also diversify my investments geographically. That way I'm not just investing in U.S. and Canadian equities. The U.S. is not the only market, after all. A strong portfolio will therefore avoid only being in the U.S. or another single geographic market.

While I'm thinking now about exposure, I haven't forgotten the 5 criteria we went over earlier. Those criteria are useful, in general. They help me avoid companies which are obvious losers.

I would therefore advise you to use both the general criteria and the specific process. Let them work together, providing you with a full view of possible investments.

If you were to look at companies in the ways I've described, you'd probably be drawn to McCormick. McCormick is a captivating company because it's "perfect" on so many fronts. If you're looking for a company to buy and collect dividends from forever, while also getting a tremendous appreciation on the stock, you really can't do much better.

McCormick is the largest spice company in the world, with a history going back to 1889. It makes spices, a product that's easy to transport and relevant to people around the globe. As a company McCormick has extremely high barriers to entry, dozens of well-established brands, and high profit margins generating a high amount of free cash flow. On top of that, the company has a long history of not only paying dividends, but also steadily increasing those dividends, uninterrupted over decades.

McCormick is a prime example of the kind of company you want in your portfolio. One that passes all of our tests for a "quality company". Passing with flying colors too.

In contrast to McCormick, an example of a company to avoid - at least based on my investing criteria - is Tesla. The company is led by Elon Musk and known for manufacturing premium electric cars.

Tesla makes a great product and seems like a great company. But as an investor, what matters are its financials. And in that area, Tesla is a bad company. It's priced to perfection. Some have even declared it to be a kind of house of cards.

I'm not sure on that last part, the house of cards. But I do believe Tesla's not worth investing in. Why invest in such a company when you can buy something more stable and predictable like McCormick. The situation is comparable to being offered $100 cash in an envelope today or a chance for the prize behind "Door #2".

In twenty years.

Pick the cash. And skip Tesla. Your chances of getting a return on Tesla are too uncertain at this point. Buy McCormick or another stable performer like Apple.

Tesla may end up becoming a great investment. Years from now. But at the moment, it's not. Not when its stock is horrifically inflated, trading at 64 times earnings. (By comparison, healthy, massively profitable companies like Johnson & Johnson and Apple are trading at 18 and 10 times earnings respectively.)

Tesla raises the broader question of whether you want to invest in potential. Taking a major risk on any company that talks big, but has yet to deliver true results?

You could, with Tesla and others, though I wouldn't recommend it. Not when you could invest in a proven, reliable stock like McCormick. Take Tesla, for example, and the company's stock is likely to wreck your portfolio, rather than spicing it up, as McCormick's would.

The process of picking stocks like McCormick, for the dividends you'll earn, is called dividend growth investing. We've explored it over the course of this chapter. From our discussion, you can see that dividend growth investing allows you to build a custom portfolio, made of companies you pick and choose. This form of investing also costs less on a yearly basis and produces a greater return than methods like mutual funds.

Dividend growth investing is not, however, without its drawbacks. The primary drawback is that it requires more time than index investing. You'll need to spend time adding each company to your portfolio. Unlike index investing, you won't be able to simply grab an entire index with multiple companies inside.

Still, once you've taken the time and added a company to your portfolio, there's little else to do. Apart from monitoring your holdings and buying more stocks as needed.

After your portfolio of dividend growth investments is set up, it will work for you. The analogy I use here is tenants paying rent in an apartment building.

Right now, my portfolio resembles a 30-unit apartment building. One of the units is occupied by a "couple" named Johnson & Johnson. I think they're in the healthcare industry. Above them in another unit is an "elderly" tenant named McCormick. He's been around forever and everyone knows him.

McCormick, Johnson & Johnson, and the other tenants in my apartment building are all paying a quarterly rent. They all pay on time, every single quarter, so I have no reason to evict anyone.

I know that it might be more profitable, perhaps temporarily, to turn my apartment building into a casino. But that would mean losing my tenants and the reliable "rent" they pay me each quarter. I'd also be squandering all of the work and research that went into setting up my apartment building. And can you imagine the environment in a casino? The constant chaos and the uncertainty of whether you'll actually make money.

No thanks! I'll stick with my apartment building and its quiet, reliable tenants.

That's all analogy, by the way. I don't actually own an apartment building. Yet the situation with my stocks is no different than tenants in an apartment. In both cases, we're focused on reliable passive income, following a long-term investor's mindset.

Reliable as dividend payments are, there's something you can count on even more. It goes with death, as one of life's two certainties.

Taxes.

Your investments produce income, which is then subject to taxes. This means you must understand where to place your investments, so as to minimize taxes (legally!) and maximize your returns. I'm no CPA, so I can't give you the exact "legal eagle" specifications of taxes in investing.

What I can tell you is that your taxes will be based on where you specifically hold your investments. Typically, investments can be held in 3 main places - a cash account, a TFSA, and an RRSP.

A cash account is exactly what it sounds like. It's an account with cash which you use to buy investments. But it's also a fully taxable account. Unlike in a TFSA or an RRSP, any dividends or interest that you earn every year are taxable.

A TFSA is what we Canadians call a tax-free savings account. If you're reading this "south of the border" (in the U.S.), you'll recognize a TFSA as equivalent to a Roth IRA.

No matter what you call it, this account type allows you to grow your investment income tax-free. You cannot deduct the annual contribution from your income in the TFSA/Roth IRA. Yet the income in the account (from investments) grows tax-free and you can withdraw it tax-free too.

Knowing the advantages of a TFSA/Roth IRA, I recommend it as the place for your stocks with the most growth potential. Spend a small amount of your "play money" on high-growth companies and put them there. That way, all the capital gains will be sheltered and, more importantly, these gains can be withdrawn tax free.

I've personally done this with companies like Under Armour and Google. Such companies don't pay dividends but they're high-growth "A-Players", so they still deserve a spot in my TFSA. Plus, as a company matures, they'll eventually start to pay dividends. This is what happened with Apple and Gilead (the "Apple" of biosciences). Those companies matured and decided to reward shareholders with dividend payments.

The third place where you can hold investments is in an RRSP. This stands for a registered retirement savings plan. With an RRSP, you pay less taxes initially because the annual contribution is deductible from your earned income. All growth is tax sheltered too. Yet when you withdraw funds from the account, they'll be fully taxable at your marginal tax rate.

Wondering how you should get started with any of these account types?

Ideally, you should "max out" (i.e. contribute up to your allowable limit for the year) your TFSA and RRSP each year. But this can be difficult when you're first starting out and have a limited income.

If you can't contribute to both account types, choose one based on your income. A salary of $50K or less per year would mean you're better off contributing to your TFSA. Let's say for instance that you can only save $5,000 per year and contribute it to one - then a TFSA would be the better bet. In contrast, if you're earning over $50K per year and still have to choose, an RRSP will be superior.

These are rough guidelines, though, and you should talk to your tax advisor for full certainly on this.

Another recommendation on these account types is to take advantage of any pension or company RRSP where your employer matches your contribution. Always take advantage of these first.

Your company could, for instance, allow you to put in $10K and then match it with their own funds. In this case, you should put in the maximum (i.e. $10K). Be mindful, however, that some pensions put their investors' money into overpriced mutual funds.

Mutual funds? You already know how "great" your returns will be in one of those. Check with your employer to make sure you're not headed for a disaster like this.

Another thing you should check on is the limits for each contribution type.

The annual limit on how much you can put in your TFSA has changed over the years. From 2009 to 2012, the limit was $5,000. It then climbed to $5,500 in 2013, before skyrocketing to $10,000 in 2015. And it's now back to $5,500 as of this year, 2016.

The limit for RRSP contributions (how much you can put in) has also changed steadily. In 2013, the limit was $23,820. The limit has increased every year since then, to its current level of $25,370 in 2016. And the RRSP limit is expected to increase yet again in 2017 to $26,010.

Are all these numbers making your head spin?

If so, I'm not surprised. It can all seem confusing. That's why I recommended hiring a good accountant. Let them do your taxes and help you manage your records.

Of the records you have, keep them well-organized. This is essential both for yourself and in the rare event that you get audited. I personally do this by having a tax folder for all of my investment properties. You'll want to keep records with folders or through your own system. But do keep records!

You have to pay taxes. No question. Even if you don't want to.

Rather than focus on taxes, I recommend focusing on those financial matters you do have a say in. In this area, I see four specific things, which I would describe as "levers". These levers allow you to command greater levels of financial success.

The first lever is your savings rate. How much you personally save. Saving is a lever because it gives you the capital to get in the game and invest. Without such capital, you can't play. Even if you want to.

It's like wanting to join a baseball game without having the right gear. You can borrow the gear from someone, if you're lucky, but then they'll need it back. And you might have other obligations to that person too. Whether it's baseball gear or money, get your own. Then you can step up to the plate and confidently take your best swing.

As an investor, savings are how you do it. You can either cut back on your spending or earn more. Then, as you have money, save fifteen to twenty percent of it. Frankly, the more you can save, the better. It's all going toward your ability to invest.

After your savings rate, the second level is what type of investments you put your money into.

What type? I say real estate - with quality properties - and dividend producing companies. Both types of investments produce consistent income for you while you're holding them. The consistency of this income allows you to focus elsewhere. You can enjoy life. Or look for other unique investment opportunities.

In the latter case, with looking for opportunities, this relates to the third of my "levers". Lever three is the ability to gather investments, packing them together to form a "snowball". When you create a "snowball", you build a portfolio that generates massive returns.

You can have your "snowball", but it takes time. Time will do the heavy lifting for you, creating a mighty portfolio if you let it. In this way, it's not hard to produce a strong portfolio on very humble beginnings. You just need to be patient. Stay committed to packing your investments together and you'll one day have a "snowball".

It's helpful here to also think of your portfolio like a bar of soap. The more you handle it, the smaller it gets. If you scrub and scrub that soap, you'll soon have nothing left. So too with your portfolio. If you "scrub" it, continually messing with your investments - you'll soon have a tiny portfolio.

The last of my financial levers is keeping your investment costs as low as possible. High costs can cripple your hopes of success as an investor. Therefore, it's important for you to keep them low at, pardon the pun, all costs. That means, for example, not churning your real estate portfolio. As we discussed in earlier chapters, it's rarely - if ever - cheap to get out of real estate. So you can't expect to get ahead by jumping in and out of owning properties.

You also won't get ahead by paying any of the investment fees I covered in this chapter. Those fees aren't as bad as in real estate. But they'll still nibble away at your progress, putting a cap on just how far you can go.

Keeping your investment costs as low as possible is the last of my financial levers. Alongside those levers, let me add three psychological levers. These are things you can control mentally.

The psychological levers were impressed upon me when I began my journey as a real estate and stock investor. During those early years, I reached out to those further along. People who had achieved the kind of investment success I hoped to one day have.

Many of them were gracious enough to share their advice with me. At the time, it humbled me and greatly contributed to my early success. Today, their example is a prime motivator for me in writing this book. I feel a similar desire to help others who are just getting started.

Anyone beginning today will likely find for themselves what I discovered in my conversations years ago, with successful investors. Then and now, those who rise succeed on a large scale because of three things. These are what I've called psychological levers.

The first is attitude. Always having a positive, can-do attitude. Always believing you can accomplish a task and approaching that task with unstoppable, unwavering will. If you can do that, you'll have a strong lever for commanding success in investing and life overall.

Your attitude must be accompanied though, with focus. This was the second of the psychological levers I discovered in talking with successful investors. Focus means being able to devote yourself passionately to a task with 100% concentration. You stay present, in the moment, when completing a task. It's what athletes call 'being in the zone'. You can't necessarily enter this state all the time. But you should practice and work on achieving it as often as possible. For focus, to the best of your abilities, will steadily drive you toward results and achievement.

To have focus, you'll need three ingredients. You must have these three ingredients to focus on anything, whether it's one of your life goals or a simple task like reading a book.

The vital three for focus, are acceptance, enjoyment, and enthusiasm. Acceptance allows you to accept that you're doing a task and not quit. Enjoyment then further commits you to the task, since you actually like performing it. When that enjoyment combines with a goal or vision you can work towards - however small that might be; it becomes enthusiasm. Enthusiasm comes from the greek "Enthousiazen", meaning to be possessed by a god. And not surprisingly, those who are enthusiastic can focus to an extent that often seems god-like.

The third psychological lever, accompanying focus and attitude, is a lack of worry. Worry is wasted energy. Successful investors recognize this. They avoid worry, enabling them to move through life energetic and unencumbered by fear.

We're now at the end of this chapter. As we wrap up the discussion, I want to bring you back to thoughts of investing. That was the main topic in this chapter. So let's end with this parting thought on investing: It's not that complicated.

Honestly.

Investing simply comes down to buying the right assets (real estate and stocks) and holding them for long periods of time. And that's basically it. You don't need to take a huge risk like quitting your day job. Nor do you have to play the nerve-wracking, confusing game with traders on Wall Street. It's so much easier and simpler than any of that.

We've seen just how elementary it is, both in this chapter and in the others throughout this book. Follow what you've read in those chapters, for 25 years or more and you'll have an excellent chance of becoming a millionaire.

I say "an excellent chance" because each of us is different and I can't speak to your individual future. But I do know that the methods in this book will work, if you give them adequate time and take consistent action.

The problem, though, is that many people can't delay their gratification. It's one of the lessons I've learned through my years in real estate and as a stock investor. I'm going to be sharing those lessons with you in the next chapter. I'll also be offering some unique insights on where I believe real estate is headed. My lessons and insights will both be useful to you in rounding out your education on financial independence.

It's all waiting for you in the next chapter, Chapter 8.

Come along for the ride!

Eight

Predictions, life lessons and advice

"Don't let the fear of the time it will take to accomplish
something stand in the way of doing it. The time will
pass anyway, we might as well put that passing time to
the best possible use."

- EARL NIGHTINGALE, INSPIRATIONAL SPEAKER

"I have never met a Real Estate investor who in the long
run had any regrets in buying a property. I have met
hundreds who regretted selling."

- OWEN BIGLAND

■ ■ ■

I have a confession to make.
This book's original title was "How to Get Rich...In Twenty-five Years
or More."

I went with a different title, though, because let's face it - few people
would read a book on getting rich in twenty-five years. You might have.
But apart from yourself, we can probably count the number of other read-
ers on one hand.

Why would the original title attract so few people? Simple. The premise is just not appealing. It's like a health book entitled, "How to Stay Fit... With Grueling Exercise and a Strict Diet". A book with that title wouldn't have a prayer on the market. And neither would this one, had its title promoted a twenty-five year road to riches.

Book titles are proof of what we discussed at the end of Section Five, on the inability to delay gratification. It's hard enough to push gratification beyond a day, a week, or even a month. But twenty-five years? Don't even go there. It's the ultimate in wishful thinking.

Unless you have a vision.

That's my goal here, in this final chapter. Before we ride off into the proverbial sunset, I want to leave you with the means to build your vision of the future. This vision will allow you to withstand the test of time. Whether that's twenty-five years. Or perhaps a bit sooner, depending on your own circumstances.

To build your vision, this chapter will focus on two areas. First, I'll offer you my predictions on where real estate is headed. With those predictions, you'll have a sense of what to look forward to as a real estate investor. And if you have things to look forward to, it'll be easier for you to delay gratification, stay focused and envision a bright future.

In addition, I'll also help you build your vision by supplying some of my own, broader life lessons. These life lessons come from having spent years in the "trenches", as a real estate and stock investor. The goal in providing them is to give you a strong foundation on which to stand as you look to the future. With such a foundation, it'll be easier for you to delay gratification and enjoy your twenty-five-year ride to wealth.

Getting started, here are my predictions on what the future holds for real estate.

First, I see units with no parking becoming far more common. This means people who reside in condos pay only for living space. A parking space is not included with the unit.

That's a bad deal for anyone who must have a car in order to live. But if you don't need a car - or are willing to give yours up - it's highly appealing. Without a car, you pay only for a unit - saving thousands of dollars in the process. And with those savings, living in the heart of a major city becomes much more affordable.

At the moment, I'm seeing this trend take root in Vancouver, along with other cities like Toronto, San Francisco, and Portland. In all of these cities, a rising class of millenials wants to live in the downtown core. But with their income, and debts like student loans, it's just not feasible. Unless, of course, they give up the $600-800 per month that it costs to have a car. Then it becomes possible to afford a unit at $1,900 or more per month. Seeing the millenials' attitude, property developers have begun offering more "car-less" units.

Property developers have also begun dedicating prime parking spaces to car sharing. This means, for example, that a new condo in Vancouver may have three parking spots exclusively for ZipCar vehicles. Here, the parking spaces would only be available for those using ZipCar - a pay-by-the-hour car rental service. Placing ZipCar at the property would be a major draw for "car-less" residents. The reason is that ZipCar empowers the "car-less", in cases when they absolutely must drive.

ZipCar, along with competitors like GoCar and Turo, are one option for the "car-less". Another option is the on-demand ride service, Uber. Uber enables you to book a reliable ride anywhere with just the tap of an app button. Uber also costs less than a traditional taxi and payment is completely cashless. While you may not want to use it for everything, the fact that Uber exists means there's now even less reason to own a car.

City planners have made it easier to go "car-less" too, by providing more streets with bike lanes - especially in core downtown areas. With the lanes, it's now easier to give up your car and travel around a packed city by bike.

Personally, I'd even go so far as to predict the bike will become "the new car" in large urban areas. It makes sense given the movement toward bike lanes, car sharing programs, Uber, and car-less units.

Whether bikes ultimately replace cars remains to be seen. But you should at least take note of what's going on. It's an important insight to have as you begin renting out property.

Your prospective tenants may very well be millenials. Assuming they are, you'll need to understand what they value. If it's cars, then yes, include parking in the unit you're renting out. But if your millenial renters value experiences, like living in a city, over possessions like cars; your rental arrangement should reflect that.

Another trend you should be aware of is the movement toward smaller, more efficient condos, and even eventually, "micro condos".

Looking at it, I see a few forces driving this trend. First, land in cities is only getting more expensive, while building costs continue to rise. As a result, the only way developers can continue to create "affordable" city housing is to shrink their units.

At the same time, millenials - as noted before - are looking for experiences, rather than a huge place to live. And, in a similar vein, there's a growing embrace of minimalism.

Minimalism, for the "uninitiated", is a philosophy of purposely living on less. The idea is that "less is more" and that you can "liberate" yourself by simplifying life down to its essentials.

In real estate, minimalism means recognizing that you don't need a five thousand square foot house. A smaller condo will suffice.

You don't have to be a philosopher, though, to appreciate smaller condos. This new style of development also works for those who might otherwise find a major city "unaffordable".

In the latter case, a city like Vancouver could seem "unaffordable" if you only wanted a house. Downsizing, on the other hand, to a smaller condo would change the game. Then, you'd be able to live in the city, paying perhaps half of what the house would have cost.

Excited about smaller condos? I am. In my opinion, this trend will only continue, in light of all the driving forces mentioned. Eventually, I see some condos shrinking from the current size of just over five hundred square feet (for a one bedroom) to around three-hundred square feet. At the new size, some condos will cease to have an enclosed bedroom and become studio-like "micro condos".

Not everyone will choose to live in a micro unit, of course. On the other end of the spectrum, families for example, will be demanding units much larger. They'll probably want units at least four times the size of a micro condo. Developers, in turn, are likely to continue building units of that size or greater to meet the demand from families. Yet some developers will probably continue shrinking the size of condos. I predict they'll do so in deference to the demands of younger, first-time buyers. For this latter group, a micro unit of only three hundred square feet might be seen as quite desirable.

Nonetheless, even with all this talk of condos shrinking, I'd advise you to remember the importance of quality. No matter how no-frills, minimalist, and "simple" people choose to live; buying quality will never go out of style.

To understand why quality will "never die", consider men's dress shoes. If you need them, you can buy a pair practically anywhere. Men's dress shoes can be found, for instance, at your local "big box" store. Walmart, Costco, Target - take your pick. Whichever you choose, you'll find a pair of black dress shoes for approximately $35-40 (USD). At first glance, these shoes look presentable and worth purchasing.

Hang on a minute, though.

Before you buy dress shoes at the "big box" store, pay a visit to a higher-end store like Nordstrom's. There, you'll find men's dress shoes from designers like Ferragamo and Bruno Magli.

Designer dress shoes will set you back roughly $450-550 (USD). But then is the purchase really a "setback"? To answer that, think for a moment about what you're paying for.

Initially, it seems you're paying only for a pair of men's dress shoes. Yet not all dress shoes are created equal. If they were, a designer like Ferragamo couldn't justify charging hundreds of dollars more for its shoes than Walmart. Designers can only justify their prices because their shoes really are different. And the difference is quality.

Quality becomes apparent when you try on a designer's shoes. The shoes feel better and look better than the low-cost alternatives. Moreover, dress shoes from a designer typically last four to five times longer, especially if you care for them.

Now just to be clear - I'm not suggesting you spend recklessly on designer shoes. Don't go into debt over a pair of shoes you can't afford. But if you can afford them, you owe it to yourself to buy quality dress shoes.

You'll find such shoes at a store like Nordstrom's, especially in July. July is when Nordstrom's puts men's dress shoes on sale at thirty to forty percent off. At those savings, you can get a pair of high-quality shoes for only about $175-350 (USD). Shoes that - as we've said - feel better, look better, and last longer. All on account of their quality.

OK, that's enough of me plugging my favorite department store. And yes, I do own shares in Nordstrom's.

Thinking about all this in terms of real estate, the same principle holds true. Buying quality properties in desirable cities never goes out of style either. Quality properties that you buy (and hold!) are like the luxury shoes in our example. Regardless of what "disruptive" trends emerge, quality items will always be valued and appreciate over time.

In the case of properties, make sure that yours are located in desirable cities. By "desirable", I'm referring to major cities like Vancouver, San Francisco, New York City, and Toronto. These cities are desirable now and I predict that they will only become more so in the future.

What makes these cities appealing is their status as lively, urban hubs. In addition, for cities like Vancouver and San Francisco; there's the added "West Coast" appeal.

Living in Vancouver, I'm perhaps a bit biased in my preference toward West Coast living. But with its relaxed climate, I'd say the West is indeed the best.

I'm not alone in this belief either. Among Canadians, Vancouver - Canada's West Coast metropolis - is widely regarded as the place to live. Americans, for their part, are also looking West. They've had a long history of "California dreaming", yearning to live in a city along the U.S. section of the West Coast.

Desirable cities, especially along the West Coast, are also sought out by those outside North America. A prime example of this is with Chinese buyers. Earlier in this book, we discussed the growing number of Chinese buying real estate in North American cities. That discussion deserves to be continued now, since it's a definite trend for the future. Looking ahead, I predict that the flow of Chinese buyers will continue into both Vancouver and other desirable North American cities.

What I can't predict is when, or if, the flow will ever stop. The present situation is so unprecedented that no one can really know what's coming next. Still, from what I make of it, Chinese buyers are getting their money out of China and putting it into North American real estate. North American real estate, in desirable cities, is seen as inherently stable. More stable than comparable properties in China or elsewhere overseas.

Chinese buyers matter to you, as a real estate investor, for two primary reasons. First, from a purely business perspective, they may be your competition. You could be located in North America, yet competing with parties in China to buy a given property. Also, with Chinese buyers involved in North American real estate, you may find yourself selling property to them. In this second case, you'd need to be aware of cultural differences, perhaps handling the sale differently too.

A final prediction I'll make here is that there will continue to be a movement toward living and working in city centers. Unlike in earlier decades, we're now seeing a "flight" back into urban areas. This is driven by the lack of space for new infrastructure. Cities simply do not have room for more highways and bridges. As populations continue to rise, transportation to and from cities now takes longer than ever. The result is that a thirty-minute drive to work, for example, might now take an hour and thirty minutes. Each way.

Who wants to spend three hours in the car every day? Some commuters might. But a growing number would rather forgo the commute by living in the city center. Life there means no commute to work, plus the freedom to walk more.

Should you live in a city center? It's certainly one way to spend less time, overall, on work. But if you're thinking only of spending less time on work, why focus on just the commute? Why not structure your life so you don't even need a job? Do that and it ceases to matter where you live.

If you want that kind of freedom, you need to become financially independent. We've seen how to do it throughout this book, with strategies of real estate, index investing, and dividend growth investing. As we wrap things up now, I want to give you those life lessons I promised earlier. Follow these lessons and you'll be able to patiently execute the strategies and become financially independent.

The first lesson I'd like to share is that money won't buy you long-term happiness. It's a cliché, I know. Yet it's true nonetheless.

The problem, though, is that the cliché doesn't say what exactly will buy you happiness. Guess the philosophers never thought of that.

You don't have to be a wise old sage, however, to know the truth. It's really quite simple. Freedom, defined as "calling your own shots" in life, is what will bring you happiness. Being free means not having to answer to anyone. You can, for example, wake up on a Monday morning and decide to spend an entire week not working.

In place of work, you might instead read an exciting book. Or, if TV shows like "Game of Thrones" are your thing, you could spend the week watching all of a show's episodes. I'm not saying you should do this. But it would be an option for you.

So no, money doesn't buy you happiness. What it does "buy" you is freedom. And with that freedom, you can do the things which make you happy. Whether that's "binge watch" a TV show, read a book, or do something altogether different.

Freedom isn't free, though. That's something I can tell you from personal experience. In my case, as a self-employed entrepreneur, I've given up the stability of a regular paycheck. At times, on the road to financial independence, not having a "safety net" like this has been nerve-wracking. Yet I can tell you that financial independence and the freedom that it brings are well worth it.

Still, don't get the wrong idea. I've always been self-employed. So my point is not that you should necessarily quit your day job. You might need that job right now to pay your bills. I'm only saying that you'll probably have to make sacrifices in order to gain your freedom. For me, the most noticeable sacrifice has been not having a stable paycheck. For you, it might be skipping some activity on the weekends and using the time to get your real estate license.

As you work toward freedom and a life where you "call the shots", it's important to maintain balance. Balance means having a life outside of work. Doing more than just working.

Balance also means having a regular exercise program.

For me, exercise has meant hitting the gym. I've been a weight lifting enthusiast for decades. In my twenties, I even spent time in Venice, California, training at the famous Gold's Gym in Venice. You don't have to go that far, though. All you need is to do at least some exercise, three to four times per week. You could go for a twenty minute jog, do some barbell work, take a swim - anything requiring physical exertion.

Just make sure you do some kind of exercise. Otherwise your overall health will suffer, causing you to not feel well over the long-term. And if you don't feel well, what good is money? What good is the freedom that it buys you? You won't be able to enjoy any of it. Not unless you balance your life through exercise.

With exercise, let's also talk quickly about diet. It goes hand-in-hand with exercise. It's really 50% of the game. If you're not fueling your body with nutrition, any gains from the training aren't going to matter. In my case, if you could see what I spend on food, you'd be amazed. High-quality fish, fresh produce, and supplements. Yet it all counts toward my performance. When I eat right, I feel great, and am at my peak to function. The same for you with the right diet. Make sure not to lose sight of that, amid everything else we're covering.

A third form of balance is breaks and vacations. I believe you need to take breaks and vacations from work, on a regular basis. Doing so helps you to stay motivated and avoid burnout, as you advance toward your goals.

Personally, I average about four to six weeks off per year. Other people go even further. One friend I have takes at least eight weeks off per year. Every few months, he'll "recharge" with a two week vacation. To each their own, but know your limits, and then take breaks and vacations based on those limits.

A final point on being balanced is that it keeps you from "changing" for the worse, as a result of having money. If you've watched entertainment news of any form, you're probably familiar with this idea. The notion that money negatively "changes" people. To keep yourself from "changing", I recommend building a life that's about more than just making money. That way, as the money does come, it won't be the only major thing on your mind. You could also, for example, be looking forward to going down to California and hitting Gold's Gym in Venice. I know I look forward to that. Working out, staying in shape, and eating healthy does it for me, and I'd imagine something else does it for you. Whatever it is, you need it as an additional focus to ensure you lead a balanced life. That's how you keep from "changing", no matter how much money you earn.

Eventually, you'll attain money and the financial independence that it brings. When you do, I would encourage you to avoid becoming idle. Spend a week watching "Game of Thrones", if you must, but don't lapse into long-term idleness. Keep exploring and learning new things.

That's easier than you might expect too. As an investor, you'll have infinite opportunities to learn about new ideas and companies. I've found this to be true when researching stocks to buy. Who knew, for example, that Tesla's profitability lagged far behind their image in the media? Or that spice companies like McCormick were so insanely profitable? I would never have guessed either. Such insights have come, though, as a result of continued learning. A continual effort to better understand the world and how to engage it.

That being said, how you want to spend your time and money is ultimately up to you. I'm personally not into fancy things. In addition, I've always practiced living within my means. But if that's not your preference and you can attain financial independence without it - more power to you.

A fourth life lesson I want to share is to work for yourself, and for others.

What?

Isn't that a contradiction? You can't work for yourself while also working for other people.

Actually you can. Let me explain.

When I say work for yourself, I'm advocating self-employment. Maybe not immediately, while you still need your day job. But eventually, once you reach the point where real estate and stock investing "liberate" you.

Self-employment is inherently preferable because your potential and rewards are unlimited. Compare that to a nine-to-five job, where your potential is capped by a salary. Plus, think about what becomes of the work you do. You pour your heart and soul into work that benefits your employer. The employer pays you of course, yet they are still ultimately the true winner.

As I mentioned earlier, I've always been self-employed. The idea of working for someone else and having them ultimately benefit has never appealed to me. Early on, I was self-employed with my own paper route. Over the years, I then worked a variety of other ventures, up to my present ones in real estate and stock investing. Each experience has left me convinced that self-employment - again, once you can afford to do it - is the best long-term choice.

Yet I also believe it's important to work for others too. Not in the sense of employment. But rather in the sense of giving back.

In giving, I can't exactly donate a wing to a hospital or give billions to the U.N. like Ted Turner. Still, you don't have to make such giant contributions to give back in a meaningful way. You could, for instance, share your knowledge on a topic with others who are just starting out. That's been my goal with this book. I also share my knowledge each week, covering real estate developments on my YouTube video blogs at YouTube.com/OwenBigland.

As you give back, I recommend being equally generous with yourself. This is the next of my life lessons - don't shortchange yourself.

Shortchanging yourself means a few things.

For starters, it means being "penny wise and pound foolish" when it comes to deals. I've learned this the hard way on a number of occasions. In one case, about ten years ago, I was on the buying side of a real estate deal. The deal was for a property that would have been perfect in my portfolio. Yet I let it go over about $5,000 to $6,000. In my haste to "save", I went and bought a different property. With twenty-twenty hindsight, though, I recognize that the original property was the better buy. I should have maintained the long-term investor's mindset and not gotten caught up over a two to three percent price difference. That difference might have seemed significant initially, but it would easily have become "peanuts" over the long haul.

Shortchanging yourself also means not paying yourself first. When you pay yourself first, you take a portion of whatever you earn and put it first into your bank account. Then whatever money is left over can be used on purchases like clothes or entertainment. Simple right? And easy too, when you start early. If you can get in the habit of paying yourself first at a young age, it becomes all you know. That's not to say you can't successfully acquire the habit later in life. It's just harder. For time is not on your side when it comes to paying yourself first, or investing. Start as soon as you can, to avoid pain down the road.

Then there's not aiming high enough. People often shortchange themselves by aiming far lower than they should. An example would be a blogger I see who saves 80% of their income. Sorry, but that's just too much. Anyone who does that is living to save, rather than saving to live. The money gets put aside sure, yet at what cost? It's hardly a life.

The goal of the blogger I mentioned is to make their lower-than-low income go far. Save $18,000 per year, for example, and one day never have to work again.

Yeah it's possible to do that. Eating canned food, never traveling, and certainly never raising a family. The question is, do you want to? Or would you rather aspire to bigger things? Aiming higher in life.

When you aim higher financially, you look for ways to increase your income and cash flow. You grow your finances, as opposed to shrinking them inward. This isn't to suggest you should live beyond your means. You never want to expand so much that it leads you into a spiral of paycheck-to-paycheck living. But simultaneously, you should avoid the trap of excess frugality. That will only lead you to aim too low, shortchanging yourself.

A fourth way I define "shortchanging yourself" is trying to take short-cuts on getting advice. Taking shortcuts means not filtering who you're listening to and not taking the time to seek out true experts. I was guilty of both early on. Starting out, my tendency was to listen to the wrong types of people. I'd fill my head with the opinions of traders on TV, rather than actual investors.

Fortunately, I was able to snap out of it as I progressed in my career. But you could easily make the same mistake. Especially today where "experts" don't even need to show their faces. At least the bad advice I got early on was from people who had to show their faces on TV. But today? The "experts" can pontificate anonymously, hiding on blogs behind silly aliases. For that reason, it's more important than ever to think about who you're getting your opinions from.

Don't shortchange yourself in this area. Probe instead into the background of each person giving you advice. Are they an anonymous blogger without a tangible track record? Or is the person giving advice a renowned, self-made millionaire? I'll leave it up to you who to take advice from. But I'd suggest taking it from the latter.

I'd also suggest aligning yourself with people who have the same overall goals and philosophies as you. These are the ones who will be most helpful in advising you when you need it. Of the people I've aligned myself with, the most influential has been my father. While we were already aligned in the sense of being family, my father has also been tremendously helpful in advising me on real estate. As a realtor of over forty years, it's safe to say he knows a thing or two about the profession. From him, I've learned specific real estate principles along with general ideas like the value of hard work.

Apart from my father, I've also aligned myself with various people and authors. Of these, I'd be remiss not to mention Warren Buffet. Buffet is a fellow dividend growth enthusiast. He's also a staunch believer in choosing stocks you can understand, even if they're boring. Alongside Buffet,

I've also aligned with and been influenced by Vanguard's Jack Bogel. Bogel has spoken widely on the need to buy entire indexes and hold them for decades.

While we're talking about people to align yourself with, I'd recommend - in general - aligning yourself with those who are self-motivated and competitive. I always have. It's come from my earliest years in the gym. Being around like-minded people, shaped my thinking profoundly for the better.

Do this and you'll find it easier to stay focused and motivated too. The reason is that you'll have less negative, counterproductive talk to tune out. Those in your circles won't be saying such things.

Not that you won't be completely free of negativity or criticism. It's bound to surface at some point. When you do face it, my recommendation is to think about where your critics are coming from. Most of the time, your critics will be those who haven't had much success in their own life or career. Their criticisms are therefore intended to drag you down or put you "in your place". Stand up for yourself, but recognize that you can't force others to see things your way. If a critic or other person doesn't agree with your vision or want success, that's their decision. Success is an "inside job", a result of the individual and their own internal drive.

Speaking of success, it's only possible when you get in the market and stay in. That's the sixth life lesson I want to share.

Good things happen when you buy quality assets and enter the market. I see this every day in just Vancouver's real estate market alone. Last week, for example, an article came out describing the incredible gains of Vancouver real estate owners. According to the article, Vancouver's home owners made more just by sitting on their real estate ass(ets) than the rest of the city did by working. The article then included the story of a homeowner in East Vancouver who made over $300,000 in the past twelve months by doing nothing but sitting on their real estate. They've done this because the market has gone up over 30% in the last twelve months.

Not bad, right? It's the smart way to make money. And proof of the good things that happen just by getting in and staying in the market.

Interestingly, though, the article acted like the homeowner it profiled was somehow not entitled to his return. Like he cheated.

Reading that, I first wondered if this story had been reprinted from The Onion, a satirical newspaper. Or if it had been written by a comedian. Neither turned out to be the case though. This article wasn't trying to be funny. The reporter really was disdainful of the homeowner's returns.

Seeing that, I wished I'd been interviewed for the story too. If only they'd asked me for thoughts on the "unjust" returns.

The Reporter: "Knowing about their returns, how do you sleep at night?"

Me: "Simple, I don't drink coffee after 2 PM."

My point would be that I don't feel any pangs of uninformed, media-induced guilt. To me it's not a surprise at all that someone could passively earn so much off real estate investment. My shock instead is at how few people understand this.

The article's author is evidently one such person. They don't understand that this is how it's supposed to work. If you, like the homeowner in the story, get in the market, acquiring and holding assets in the same way - you create the potential to see similar gains. Your gains may not come immediately and they may be not as dramatic. But the gains will come eventually, causing you to get ahead.

You won't see any gains, however, if you do what the article implies is the "respectable" way - working for a paycheck. Forget that advice and get your money working for you, through real estate and equity (stocks).

And, as an added recommendation, I suggest you look at articles like this differently. Avoid getting swept up in the feelings of "injustice" or "outrage" that an article like this seeks to create. Think instead about the lessons that can be learned. Think to yourself, "What can I learn or gain from watching this success story?" Do that and you'll see opportunity where others cannot.

At this point, I want to leave you with one last life lesson. Since we've discussed weighty topics throughout the text, let's end on a light note. Think of this last lesson, then, as the dessert after the hearty main courses we've had. And, in the spirit of dessert, it's only fitting that this final lesson would be about desserts. Sugar cookies, actually.

The lesson is based on a commencement speech by William McRaven. McRaven is a distinguished former U.S. Navy four-star admiral. During his career, he served as commander of various special operations divisions. He also became famous for leading the mission that took down terrorist Osama Bin Laden

In his commencement speech at the University of Texas in 2014, McRaven talks about "sugar cookies". The term comes from Navy SEAL training.

During their training, SEAL candidates awaken at 4:30 AM each morning. They must then make their bunk and uniform with absolute perfection. An inspection soon follows, as commanding officers look for any mistakes.

Given the importance of the tasks, SEAL candidates are unlikely to have made mistakes. Yet even if they haven't, commanding officers can still pick a candidate out at random. The given candidate will be criticized, despite having done nothing wrong. Then they'll be commanded to remove their uniform, run into the surf, and roll in the sand for five minutes. The resulting look is what's called a "sugar cookie". The unfortunate SEAL candidate must then spend the next twelve hours of grueling training in this humiliating, highly uncomfortable state - cold, wet, and covered in sand.

The takeaway from McRaven's story is that this is exactly how life works. In life, even if you do everything exactly right, there will still be times when you're derailed. Life is going to make you into a "sugar cookie". Not always. But it will happen. Your job then is to roll with it. Overcome your "sugar cookie" moments to achieve success. Whether that means making the "dough" (money) or attaining other goals. If you can do that, then there will honestly be nothing stopping you from living the life you want.

■ ■ ■

Is it really time?

Time to say goodbye?

I don't know about you, but I hate goodbyes. There's just no good way to do them. You can rush the goodbye, but that feels insincere. Or you can do a long, drawn-out goodbye. But then it gets really awkward.

So let's not say goodbye. Not yet anyway.

You're now at the end of this book. But it doesn't have to be the end of our discussion.

As I mentioned, I have a video blog. It's updated regularly at YouTube.com/OwenBigland, and I'd love to get your feedback on the posts and this book.

In addition, I'm happy to take your questions or comments on what we've covered here. Feel free to contact me through my YouTube channel.

Thanks for taking time to read this book.

Best wishes till we meet again.

--Owen

My Core Holdings

S till hungry? Here's another morsel...
You know I've never claimed to be a "guru". And in that same spirit, I'm going to do now what no guru in their right mind would ever do. They'd have to be crazy.

I'm going to put all of my core holdings on display. Everything in my portfolio. Right out in the open. For your viewing pleasure.

In doing so, I hope to satisfy your appetite for further knowledge on investing.

I also hope that the list of my core holdings will be a starting point for you, rather than an end. Think of that as a disclaimer. A BIG DISCLAIMER.

I'm NOT suggesting you go out and buy this exact portfolio today. Instead, what I'm giving you is the spark for your own investment research. Take the list, recognizing that many of its stocks are now trading at 52-week and all-time highs. So these stocks may not represent a good entry point at current values.

Besides, if nothing else, don't you want the thrill of finding your own great investments? I'll tell you from experience that it can definitely get exciting when you deep-dive into research and find great buys.

Now for my core holdings...

U.S. Holdings

These stocks are primarily held in my RRSP and my US$ cash account. Most of them pay a nice dividend and, more importantly, they have continuously raised their dividends over the last 20 years or more.

Stocks - RRSP and US$ Cash Account

AAPL
JNJ
MCD
WMT
PEP
KO
GE
PG
CVX
MO
PM
DEO
UTX
UL
DOW
DIS
HSY
CL
MKC
BF-B
HON
MMM
XOM
CVS
NKE
NSRGY

I also hold stocks in my TFSA. Here, you'll find more growth-oriented stocks. Those sort of stocks make sense here because with a TFSA, all capital gains are tax-free when the stocks are sold.

Stocks - TFSA

    BRK-B
    CELG
    COST
    GOOGL
    GILD
    UA
    SBUX
    STZ

ETF Holdings (U.S.)

    VTI
    VIG
    SPY
    DTD

Canadian Stocks

Oh Canada! Our national anthem. And my reaction to the stellar performance on some of these next stocks.

Canada can definitely be a great place for investment, thanks to the Canadian dividend tax credit. That credit comes to me by keeping Canadian stocks in my CDN cash account.

Stocks - CDN Cash Account

    ENB
    RY
    TD

BMO
BNS
SLF
T
BCE
POW.TO
BAM.A
SU
NA
PWF.TO
CNR
CM
MG

ETF Holdings (Canada)

XIC
ZDV

European and Emerging Markets

When it comes to European and emerging markets, I'm certainly no George Soros. Unlike him, you won't find me impacting England's economy with my investments. Nor am I deep in the financial "wilderness" of distant lands, betting big on the "next big market". That said, I do have some holdings in European and emerging markets. Good opportunities I've found. Never hurts to shop around, right?

Holdings

VWO
VXUS
EFA

Questions & Answers

1. I hear stock market trading and real estate investment seminars advertised on the radio. Are they a good way to get started?

No, steer clear of these events. The only thing 99% of such events want you to start on is losing money. They'll do that by trying to sell you expensive training courses that flat out don't work.

If it's real estate, the course will usually be based on some kind of no-money-down scheme. If it's stocks, you'll be misled into stock trading via charts and trading software programs. Either way, the promise is a quick way to riches. But as I've told you in this book, that's not the way it works in real life.

If it were, why the **** are these people doing seminars? The reason, of course, is that the seminars themselves are the real way any of these false prophets make a profit. Don't let them sell this snake oil to you. If you want to actually achieve wealth, you won't do that with glitzy software and color-coded handouts. You will, however, get to your destination with tried-and-true action, following the blueprint I've provided in this book.

2. How can I hope to buy my first condo when the prices in Vancouver (or any major city) are so expensive? I don't have a million dollars to get started.

You don't need a million dollars to get started. Trust me. Take my city Vancouver. The one I've described as having real estate prices resembling Manhattan's. Vancouver can be expensive alright. But the city also has its affordable side. A mere thirty to forty minutes away, for example, sit one-bedroom units priced at $200K. There are also two-bedroom units priced in the mid to upper $200's.

Now to be fair, living in these units won't be the same as staying at the Four Seasons Hotel. But they do make an excellent first purchase. Think of it as starting with a Motel 6 and moving your way up from there.

But do get started. Whether that's in Vancouver, or in your own city where comparable pockets of affordability exist. The key is to get your foot in the market as soon as possible. Once you are, when the market appreciates, you'll be carried along for the ride as opposed to sitting idly on the sidelines. You'll also be owning your principal residence and accumulating all capital gains on it, tax-free.

3. On your video blog at owenbigland.com you've said you don't worry about market corrections and that you actually look forward to them in both the stock market and real estate. How are you not worried or concerned when you see the value of your portfolio go down? I know I would be worried.

I never get concerned or worried because of the way I view these corrections. In my mind, market corrections are fantastic buying opportunities. I'm still young enough to be in the accumulation stage. I also have plenty of time to hold the stock or property until its price recovers, which always happens if you give it time. Unless you're near or at retirement age (in you mid-60's or older) you should view these corrections the same way.

Think of it like your favourite store is having a 20%-off sale on all its merchandise. If you're a guy, for example, this means you can get a fancy new suit at 20%-off the full price. And for the ladies, it's like being able to buy designer shoes or a hand bag at a deep discount. Look at corrections in these terms, and you'll be as relaxed as I am.

4. I bought a pre-sale condo two years ago as an investment. It's now getting ready to complete next month. The market is up over 25% since I purchased the condo (up over $100K). I'm thinking of selling it and taking my profit.

If you sell, you're playing real estate "little league". That's because you'll pay me (or another realtor) my commission to list and sell the property for you. On a $500K condo, that's going to be approximately $17,000. Next, you'll pay capital gains taxes of approximately $20,000. There will also be other selling costs like legal and transfer fees.

Once all that's over with, you might be left with $60K. It's a nice profit, to be sure. But it's still "Little League" compared to what you'll get if you hold. Wait 20 or 25 years and your profit will be much, much greater. It'll be the big leagues compared to whatever you'd earn now.

So I suggest you stick with your original game plan. Keep the unit, put a tenant in there, and let time and compounding do all the heavy lifting for you. You and your bank account will thank me later.

5. My friend (co-worker, teacher, bowling buddy, beer league hockey teammate, etc.) tells me RRSP's are not worth it. You're going to get taxed on it in the end anyway.

Your friend's right. Once you start withdrawing the funds at retirement, the funds received each year will be taxed at your marginal tax rate.

Nonetheless, there are still two compelling reasons to contribute to an RRSP. First, you get the tax deduction for the contribution each year. This means if you're in a 35% tax bracket during your working years, it's like contributing 65 cents on each dollar. The second advantage is all the growth during your working years accumulates tax free.

6.   I want to sell my investment condo with my tenant still occupying the unit.

No, just no! This is classic "penny-wise, pound-foolish" thinking. The kind of thinking that serious investors avoid.

If it's any comfort, though, you're not alone. About 7 out of 10 people fall prey to this same mistake.

I encounter some of them in my work as a realtor. A condo owner, for example, will call me and want to list their property for sale. With tenants in it.

Hearing this I immediately ask them a few questions. Questions you need to ask too when looking to sell a property with tenants already in place.

First, what is the nature of the tenancy? By nature, I mean is the tenancy on a fixed term lease or a month-to-month lease.

Fixed term means that the tenant is leasing the condo for a set length of time (six months, one year, etc.).

If the lease is fixed term, I then ask how many months are left on the lease. The condo owner may reply that their tenant has a month left. Perfect. Give your tenant notice now that you won't be renewing their lease. And call me in a month when the tenant is out. We can resume our discussion then.

It's not always that easy, though. Sometimes the tenant will have six months or more left on their fixed term lease. Here, I'd still advise the condo owner to wait and contact me later, once the tenant is out.

But I may not be as persuasive to the owner as Benjamin Franklin. Or Ulysses Grant. Or whoever else is on the cash they envision making from a quick sale of the condo.

Besides, why wait?

Because it won't be quick or easy. Not unless you're incredibly lucky. That's the irony of trying to sell a condo with a tenant still in it. It typically ends up taking far longer than without an existing tenant. Not to mention requiring more effort.

One reason is that nearly 90% of potential buyers don't want your tenant. They want the property to be theirs and theirs-alone, at least initially. So when most potential buyers see your tenant will come "along for the ride" (and not in our sense!), it immediately scares them off.

The buyers who might then be interested are few and far between. This puts you in a position where you have to take whatever offers you can get. Provided you can even get any.

If you want to avoid this situation, it's simple really. Get your tenant out. You can do it, as we've said, by waiting. Tell the tenant ASAP that you can't redo their lease. Then wait.

Or consider approaching your tenant about vacating sooner. In the latter case, you (as landlord) need to get a "Mutual Agreement to End Tenancy". This is a written agreement between you and the tenant on them leaving before the existing date. Ideally, you can get the tenant to leave within the next 40 to 50 days.

Regardless of what you want, though, tenants on a month-to-month lease must be given 2 full months notice. That's 2 full months from the time you get the buy offer and subjects are removed. So if, for example, that date was June 3rd, your tenant would be able to stay until September. For these are full months, not partial ones.

To have your tenant want to leave early, you'll have to pay them at least one month's rent as reimbursement. And you'll usually pay more just to sweeten the deal. The amount and terms are all negotiable.

But it'll be money well spent because you'll retain those 90% of buyers. You also won't have to work around the tenant's schedule on times for showing the place. Nor will you risk the tenant's own behavior (messiness, for example) deterring those who visit your unit. You'll be in complete control of the property, presenting it as you want.

Whew! Long answer, huh? This answer (in our Q&A) ended up far longer than expected. It's worth explaining, though, because you really don't want to make such a severe mistake. Fortunately, you're now aware that selling a property with a tenant inside is a mistake. It's almost as bad as trying to sell a used, non-luxury car with a driver (who isn't a chauffeur). Good luck!

The last thing I'll say on this is that most sellers don't even spot the error. Unlike you, most sellers (and their realtors too!) are totally unaware.

I saw this recently with a condo on the market. One with 5 months left on the tenancy. The unit was listed at $460K. And, as predicted, it stayed listed. For a long, long time.

Eventually, I made the only offer and bought the place. At a sale price of $448K, I consider this to be a good deal. But think about it from the seller's perspective. They should have gotten multiple offers and sold the property for well over its asking price.

Plus, adding insult to injury, the condo appreciated by $55,000 in the 5 months I waited for its tenant to leave. Another win for the buyer and a loss for the seller.

And the seller wasn't even aware. But you are...

7. Why would you ever want to own a company like McDonald's? People are eating healthy these days.

It's not about the fast food. Look at the fundamentals of the company. When you buy McDonald's, you're actually investing in real estate. It's a real estate company disguised behind a fast food venture.

McDonald's owns most of the real estate that its stores occupy. This is real estate is in the billions of dollars now. Suppose for example, that they have a store in Midtown Manhattan. A place built in the 1970's, where they paid half a million dollars for the lot. Today, that property can easily be worth $25 to $30 million.

Worldwide, McDonald's has thousands of cases like this. Instances where they own both the restaurant and the land, and have done so for decades. All the while, the real estate has been sitting on the books for its original value.

If the company ever spun off these real estate assets, they'd unlock tens of billions of dollars. The value of their real estate holdings would finally be realized, creating an economic tidal wave. They may never do that, but it's incredibly exciting to consider. And it only makes McDonald's - already a powerful, profitable, dividend-paying champion - all the more exciting.

8. I'm worried about _____(the election, Brexit, Zika virus, war, the economy, unemployment, oil prices, new taxes, etc, etc.) Think I'll just wait on the sidelines until this passes.

When exactly do you think it will pass? And when it does, don't you think there will be plenty of other seemingly threatening events to follow? Call me a pessimist, but I've never seen there being all "sunny skies" when it comes to real estate or stocks. Throughout my time as an investor in either area, I've always faced dark clouds hanging somewhere on the horizon. Events that seemed just as threatening as the one(s) you're anxious over now. But I've always recognized these problems for what they were. Seeing them as unnoticeable waves on the beach, rather than coast-wrecking tsunamis. If you want to succeed as an investor, you must adopt this same view. Leave the sidelines, tune out these "end of the world" scenarios, and relax. You'll not only feel better, you'll also be further along on the road toward financial independence.

9. I sold all my stock in 2009 after the crash and will never go back. I keep my money in bonds and term deposits now. It's safe.

And you were the only person to get burned in 2009....No, of course not. Lots of people got burned. Like you, many of them also have their savings now in fixed income. That might be OK if you're in your 70's and retired. But if you're in your 20's through 50's - an accumulation stage - you're losing money by being in these "vehicles".

You're losing out because your bonds are only earning 1.5%. Your term deposits or money-market accounts, in turn, are only earning anywhere from 0.5% to maybe 1%. And all the while, inflation is averaging 2.5-3%.

To illustrate your loss, here's an example. Suppose you put $1,000 into a term deposit and locked it in for a year at a 1% return.

You'd then make $10 in interest. Yay!

But if you're in the 30% tax bracket (about as low as you can get taxed), you'll automatically lose $3 in taxes. Inflation will then also have its turn at eating your money. With inflation, your $1,000 investment is now only worth about $977 per year. So your money actually becomes worth less as a result of locking it away in the term deposit.

It's like you're carrying a bucket of water, with holes in it. You drip money, instead of water. Not necessarily bad news, if you're close to your destination. Or in the money case, if you're in your 60's-70's, and retired.

But if you're young, this is CRAZY. A term deposit deprives you of growth opportunities and puts you behind in each successive year. It's about as bad as keeping your money in a coffee can or burying it in the backyard.

What you really need is to reenter the stock market. As you do, work to understand its fundamentals, so you can have faith and stay the course.

10. Buying and renting out a condo is a lot of work. Especially with so many bad tenants.

Sorry, but it's probably just you. Screen your tenants better and you won't have this problem. For more info on this see Chapter 4.

11. I want to make money flipping houses. I hear this is the way to make real money.

Who have you heard that from? If it's the experts selling seminars...well, you know how I feel about those guys.

Nonetheless, some people do make real money flipping houses. I'll admit it. Cases do exist where flipping can be quite profitable. But before you flip out over flipping, look at who's succeeding with it.

The successful flippers are overwhelmingly the experts. People who know flipping real estate like an Olympic gymnast knows flipping physically. The point being that successful real estate flippers have done it enough to achieve mastery. And in doing so, you can bet that they - like the Olympic gymnast - took plenty of falls.

Taking a "fall", as in taking a financial loss, is nearly inevitable when flipping houses. Over a long enough term. That's because flipping is dependent on the real estate market continuing to rise.

While the market rises, you can make money by acquiring and quickly turning over properties (i.e. flipping them). Yet eventually the market will have one of its natural corrections.

If this happens after you've bought a property to fix up, you're probably stuck with the place. You've paid peak price for it on the assumption that the market would continue to rise. Now, though, as prices fall, you must either sell A.S.A.P. or hold the property until the market resumes its ascent. Otherwise, you'll be taking a financial loss on what you originally paid.

Expert flippers understand the risk inherent in flipping. They also can afford to take a loss. Amateur flippers, though, usually lack such awareness or a "Plan B".

A final thought on flipping is that half of the cost is materials and half is labour. To renovate a full one-bedroom condo, for example, you'll likely spend about $40,000 total. You'll be spending around that amount because you probably aren't a contractor. So you can't do the labour required in flipping yourself. Instead, you must pay others to do the work.

If, however, you could do the labour, you would then save substantial money. Probably about $20,000 or more. With those savings, you'd be spending less to fix up your property. Meaning your expenses would decrease and your potential profit from a flip would be greater. But again, most people aren't in this position.

12. My financial advisor tells me he's been beating and outperforming the market.

I'm sure he is. But what kind of a time-frame are we talking about? Your advisor's "success" is probably just within the last year or two. Let's see them beat the market over five, ten, or fifteen years time.

If your financial advisor can consistently beat the market for a decade or more, then I stand corrected. Your particular advisor is special. But it's highly unlikely since most advisors can't do that.

What they can do - quite masterfully too - is zoom-in on a tiny sliver of the graph. Enough to show their performance beating the market.

Make sure you zoom-out whenever it looks too good to be true.

13. My financial advisor is trying to sell me mutual funds. His/her returns over the last 5 years look excellent.

Consider what we just said (for #12) about returns in the short versus long term. This tactic is used by both stock advisors and mutual fund companies. Yet neither can consistently beat the index over a long time.

In addition, after fees are deducted, you're going to lag far behind. So if somehow they did beat the odds with excellent 5-year returns, you'd still be worse off.

14. Your advice on not renting goes against what I've read in a recent book. The author of that book says you should be renting, not buying, and then investing the difference. Who should I believe?

That's kind of a loaded question. But let me try answering it objectively.

Authors like the one you're referring to appear every 6 to 7 years when a market gets hot and home prices are a record highs. They write books and go on TV, advocating you rent and save the difference. Yet if you're living in a major city today, like Vancouver or Toronto (and its U.S. equivalents), there's virtually no savings.

Why you ask? Because of interest rates. Today interest rates sit at re-cord lows, hovering around 2%. They are expected to remain low too, for at least the next decade.

This is a different ballgame, so to speak, from the 80's. Those were the days of sky-high interest rates (15% to 18%) and relatively cheap rents.

Remember that interest rates dictate how much you pay on a monthly mortgage. So in the 80's, there were cases where a monthly mortgage was much higher than a monthly rent. Cases where a person would in-deed save money by renting versus buying and having to pay the monthly mortgage.

Still, even if such opportunities did arise, only a highly disciplined per-son could have come out ahead. Most people tended to rent and spend the difference, rather than carefully investing it.

Whatever opportunities to save existed then are long gone. The 80's aren't coming back. Which is probably a good thing, given the goofy fashions (leg warmers, really?).

But if we're talking, seriously now, about 80's interest rates; those aren't coming back either. Not for a long time.

Instead, interest rates are going to stay around 2% to 3%. Lower rates mean you'll be paying far less than in the past on your monthly mortgage - were you to take out a mortgage and buy a property. Your monthly mortgage will be so low that it's really no different - in terms of money spent - than pay-ing a monthly rent.

Interest rates could hypothetically, go up again. But it would have to be way more than a casual increase. Rates would need to triple before we could even think about the possibility of saving from renting.

As proof of the lack of savings today, between renting versus buying, let's look at some raw numbers.

We'll use the numbers from an earlier example, 33 Pender Street. Where the buyer put down 20% (their down payment) on a $450,000 unit.

This down payment left $360,000 on the mortgage. At current in-terest rates, the mortgage payment is therefore $1,561.17 per month or $18,734.04 per year. That payment covers both interest ($7,810.28) and principal ($10,923.76). There are also annual maintenance fees ($4,463.04), property taxes ($1,247.98), and an additional $1,200 per year for repairs. Together, all of the payments put the total cost to own the condo at $25,645.07 per year.

After 25 years the condo will be fully paid off. If you were its owner, you would own the place with clear title. Based on conservative estimates, your condo could be worth $1.2 to $1.5 million dollars. That money would flow to you tax-free as soon as you decided to sell the condo. You could then take your tax-free proceeds of say $1.2 million and buy a basket of Canadian blue chip, dividend-paying stocks. The kind that yield 4%.

Your stocks would produce over $48,000 in annual dividend income. The $48k would float in, being taxed at a very low rate, and you'd never need to touch the principal.

At that point, perhaps you'd consider investing in another property or equities. But no matter what you did, you'd have options. Options that come with ownership.

No such options would exist after 25 years of renting. Rent and you'd pay $2,100 per month or $25,200 per year. Over the same twenty-five year span, that equates to $630,000. *Note we are not indexing this rent amount to reflect inflation and rent increases. A long term renter could easily drop 1 million dollars on rent over the next 25 years with zero to show for it.

Unfortunately, the $630K wouldn't give you anything beyond a temporary place to live. At the end of 25 years (a quarter century!), you'd still lack stability and need to find housing.

Worse yet, you'd have absolutely nothing to show for all the money you spent. The money you paid would have gone to your landlord. It would not have helped you to fully acquire the property as your own asset. An asset which you could sell to become an instant millionaire and be set for life.

No, you wouldn't have done that. By renting, you'd instead stay asset-less. Essentially giving away $630,000 over the 25-year span.

Can you see now - really see - why renting doesn't make sense? Why buying a property like the one I mentioned, on 33 Pender Street, is a far, far wiser decision?

Naturally, you do need a down payment to buy property. With the Pender Street condo, for example, you'd need to pay $90,000 up front. No getting around that.

But come on! Isn't it worthwhile? Scraping and saving today to get the down payment money. So you can be set for life, later on?

I think so. Hopefully you agree. You might even be so convinced that you're now "kicking yourself" for not starting earlier. If so, I'd encourage you to relax.

In all likelihood, you still have time. Just get started as soon as you can. Cobble together the money for the down payment, pronto. Find that cash wherever it's hiding and use it to get yourself into the market. Your money cannot begin working for you, until you do.

Never forget that your money is a "ghost ship". A crew-less vessel, silently carrying you to exciting financial horizons. This ship can't take you there, however, when you haven't invested. Without investment, it's like the ship sits in dry-dock. You need to break the champagne and get it in the water. Only then can you and your money set sail.

Recommended Resources

My book isn't the only one out there. And unlike many "experts" I'm not afraid to admit that. In fact, I want you to seek out other books. For corny as it sounds, those who read succeed. The successful ones also follow CREDIBLE websites. For your convenience, I've provided a list of such sites below, along with a recommended reading list. Read these books, visit the websites too, and you're bound to become - to paraphrase the title of a well-known book - an "intelligent investor".

Recommended Books

Think and Grow Rich by Napoleon Hill
The Snowball by Warren Buffet
The Millionaire Next Door by Thomas Stanley and William Danko
One Up On Wall Street by Peter Lynch
A Random Walk Down Wall Street by Burton Malkiel
The Strangest Secret by Earl Nightingale
What They Don't Teach You At Harvard Business School by Mark McCormack
The Power Of A Dream by Peter Legge
The Little Book Of Common Sense Investing by Jack Bogle
The Power of Now by Eckhart Tolle
How to Win Friends and Influence People by Dale Carnegie

The Magic of Thinking Big by David J. Schwartz
Tools of Titans by Tim Ferris

Recommended Websites

Seeking Alpha (seekingalpha.com)
Canadian Couch Potato (canadiancouchpotato.com)
Dividend Growth Investor (dividendgrowthinvestor.com)
Dividend Ninja (dividendninja.com)
Dividend Mantra (dividendmantra.com)
Mr. Money Mustache (mrmoneymustache.com)
Joshua Kennon (joshuakennon.com)

Made in the USA
San Bernardino, CA
13 May 2017